Ripper Notes
The American Journal
for Ripper Studies

www.RipperNotes.com

Editor:
Dan Norder
2 N. Lincoln Ridge Dr.
Apt. #521
Madison, WI 53719
        dan@norder.com

Subscriptions:
Ripper Notes is
published quarterly in
January, April, July and
October. One year /
four issue subscriptions
are $30 domestic (in the
U.S. and Canada) and
$35 overseas. Payments
by check or money
orders made out to Dan
Norder and in U.S.
funds can be sent to the
address above, or pay
with a credit card via
www.RipperNotes.com

On the cover:
• A new Jack the Ripper
action figure (image
copyright 2004 by
McFarlane Toys, used
with permission), see
News & Notes
for details.
• Mugshot of Carrie
Brown, courtesy NYC
Municipal Archives.

Back cover:
• The "McFarlane
Monsters 3 - Six
Faces of Madness"
line (also copyright
2004, see above).
• Walter Sickert's
La Hollandaise, see
News & Notes for
exhibition info.

GW00496655

July 2004 — Issue #19

Contents copyright 2004 by Dan Norder for *Ripper Notes*.
ISBN 0-9759129-0-9
Ripper Notes is published by Inklings Press.
The opinions expressed in articles and letters are those of the individual
authors and are not necessarily shared by the editor.

Introduction

Ripper Notes started out in 1999 as a newsletter of Casebook Productions but grew into a journal full of articles about all aspects of the Whitechapel murders and related topics. This April, Christopher-Michael DiGrazia stepped down as editor in order to free himself up for other projects. He, along with previous *RN* editors Christopher T. George and Sam Gafford, built the publication into one recognized by Ripper scholars and hobbyists. I have the utmost respect for what they managed to do — getting things running in the first place is the hardest part.

I took over as editor to not just keep *Ripper Notes* going, but to build it up. Some people have been quick to point out that it's easily the best American periodical on the topic (and only one, as others point out), but that label unfortunately makes it an also-ran in the minds of some. It's time to set our sights higher.

So, first up, I made some changes to the look. New logo, full color cover, perfect binding (no staples here). This issue should fit on a bookcase like it belongs there — and I think it certainly deserves it We have serious authors writing on real topics, and they should be treated as such.

Going along with that thought, there's no reason why the members of the general public shouldn't be able to order this publication through their favorite bookstore. So, as a first step toward that direction, I signed up for ISBN codes. That long number on the back cover is a standard identifier that any bookstore should be able to work with.

While you probably won't see *Ripper Notes* at a neighborhood shop anytime soon, within a month or so you should be able to special order it or find it at Amazon's online stores.

And, if we want people to order copies site unseen, it's nice for them to know a little more about what they'd be getting beforehand. The easiest way I thought of to do that was to have a theme each time around. With Wolf Vanderlinden's in-depth look at the suspects in the Carrie Brown murder in New York and some articles based upon the U.S. Ripper Conference (also originally started by Casebook Productions, by the way), "America looks at Jack the Ripper" fit.

And it seemed especially apt one after all the talk of supposed differences between Americans and the British that I kept hearing after becoming editor. I was welcomed to the "UK world of the Ripper" or asked what it was like to be an American in a British-dominated field. Others thanked me for providing an "alternative to British viewpoints." It seems to me that one's country of origin shouldn't make a bit of difference. Hey, I'm from Wisconsin and don't try to claim ownership of Jeffrey Dahmer or Ed Gein. (But then I think Ed Gein at least has already been thoroughly stolen by Hollywood anyway.)

So, let this issue serve notice: *Ripper Notes* isn't satisfied with being second best, whether we happened to be based out of the U.S. or not. It's time for serious (but friendly) competition.

- Dan Norder

Dr. Anderson at New Scotland Yard

An 1892 Interview Rediscovered

Editor's note: A few months back I asked friends and various researchers at the vintage bookshops I do business with to be on the lookout for any old documents that might relate to the Jack the Ripper case and some other related topics. I received many responses, the vast majority of which were simply books and articles containing information that has been hashed and rehashed quite thoroughly over the years. I had thought that a woodcut of Thomas Byrnes (see Wolf Vanderlinden's article in this issue) was going to be the best find. Something quite interesting found its way into my hands recently, however.

To the best of my knowledge, the following piece on Assistant Commissioner Robert Anderson, an important figure in the Ripper case, has not been previously published or referenced by modern Ripperologists. Unlike most of his existing known comments, this article was printed within only a few years of the murders.

Here are some important dates (compiled from the *Casebook: Jack the Ripper* website and Begg, Fido and Skinner's *The Jack the Ripper A-Z*) to help put the following interview into context:

1888: Dr. Robert Anderson named Assistant Commissioner of the Metropolitan Police. The canonical five victims of "Jack the Ripper" are killed.

1891: Aaron Kosminski is placed in Colney Hatch asylum.

1892: The following article.

1894: Mcnaghten Memorandum (a private police document) names a "Kosminski" as the Polish Jew suspect who was put in asylum.

1901: Anderson retires and is knighted.

1907: Anderson claims that the Whitechapel murderer "had been safely caged in an asylum."

1910: Anderson's autobiography is published. In it, he makes several important statements about Jack the Ripper:

• "And if the Police here had powers such as the French Police possess, the murderer would have been brought to justice."

• "I will merely add that the only person who had ever had a good view of the murderer unhesitatingly identified the suspect the instant he was confronted with him ; but he refused to give evidence against him."

• "In saying that he was a Polish Jew I am merely stating a definitely ascertained fact."

(Retired Chief Inspector Donald Swanson's copy of this autobiography was found many years later with notes in the margin and at the end that read, in part: "...the suspect was sent to Stepney Workhouse and then to Colney Hatch and died shortly afterwards – Kosminski was the suspect.")

Readers of the following will note that comments in this interview foreshadow the later comparisons to French police, but that no mention of an identification can be found here. Rather, Anderson says that it is "impossible to believe" that the killer was sane, which is an interesting phrase.

If Kosminski had been positively identified as the Ripper in 1891, why then is Anderson making a reference that the killer should be *believed* to be insane based upon crime scene photos and not an identification more than a year later?

Like with previous comments by police officials, the statements in the following article are sure to inspire much debate...

Representative Men at Home:
Dr. Anderson at New Scotland Yard
from *Cassell's Saturday Journal*
June 11, 1892 (pages 895-897)

LONDON'S foremost detective is a tallish gentleman in the prime of life, of precise habits, of quiet demeanour, and whose face is that of a deep student. His signature a little while since was attached to some thoughtful letters in the *Times*, a contribution to the controversy on the "Bible and Modern Criticism." The subject must have been very near to his heart, for as an author Dr. Robert Anderson – he took his LL.D. at Dublin University – is not unknown in this connection. He first published "The Gospel and Its Ministry," and next, "The Coming Prince: the Last Great Monarch of Christendom," which is illustrative of the meaning of that most celebrated of prophecies, the Seventy Weeks of Daniel, and is also a chronology of the whole period of the Jewish captivity. These works were followed by "Human Destiny," a critique upon the most forward books upon that topic; and, finally, a couple of years ago, by "A Doubter's Doubts," a treatise which was written from the standpoint of a Free Thinker, and dealt with both science and religion in that spirit. It was published anonymously, and it attracted the attention of Mr. Gladstone, who wrote to the author twice concerning it, expressing "a great deal of sympathy and concurrence" in his views, "and hoping that the writer of the volume would follow up the subject with the "same care, force, and exactitude" which in it he "had bestowed especially upon the treatment of the main argument."

Since he became a Commissioner of Police, Dr. Anderson has abandoned journalism, in which he used to dabble, but he has written upon "Criminals and Crime" in the *Contemporary;* and his article upon "Morality by Act of Parliament" was a distinct "hit."

"Care, force, exactitude," these words of Mr. Gladstone's we may well adopt in describing Dr. Anderson's characteristics. They leave their impress upon his surroundings: in the orderly arrangement of the papers which cover his desk, in the neatness of the bookshelves in the case which faces him, even in the systematic building up of the fire in the grate on principles which, if generally adopted, would abolish a great deal of fog, and in many another detail one unconsciously obtains an insight into the manner of man who courteously gives attention to his visitor.

Dr. Anderson, from what has been said, possesses that which might almost be called a dual personality. Few criminals could picture to themselves the domestic scene at 39, Linden Gardens, where the Assistant Commissioner resides quietly. Our artist, in his larger sketch, shows us the thoughtful student at home, free for the time being from the harassing duties of criminal investigation, but not so immersed in his reading as to forbid the intrusion of his little girl. Indeed, if one may guess at the truth, Dr. Anderson finds his best relaxation in the society of his children. Occasionally a cricket match at the Oval may have as great attractions to the father as it has to his sons, as a relief to the mental exercises which to an ordinary mind would seem more than severe, and in no sense a relaxation.

How came such a deep thinker and student of prophecy, Biblical chronology, science, and philosophy to enter upon his present duties? In what way are the first detectives of to-day trained? In what school must they gain experience in order to be successful? By way of answer to these questions Dr. Anderson's history is instructive.

His father was Crown Solicitor for Dublin, and his brother – the late Sir Samuel Anderson – had charge of all the State prosecutions. Thus it came about at the end of 1866 that Lord Mayo asked Dr. Robert Anderson, who was then practising at the Irish Bar, to help him in disposing of an accumulation of foreign office despatches and reports of all kinds, supposed to be extremely secret, which were stowed away unindexed and unregistered at the Chief Secretary's office. Naturally the Lord Lieutenant wished to know what these papers contained, and Dr. Anderson was asked to examine them.

"That was when I took the Queen's shilling," observes the Assistant Commissioner; "but I didn't vacate my position at the Bar; it was, on the contrary, rather benefited by these duties."

Whilst on circuit at the spring assizes in 1867, the Fenian rising took place, and 200 or 300 prisoners were marched into the yard at Dublin Castle and solemnly committed for trial on the charge of high treason. But having caught so many hares the problem was how to cook them. The Attorney General telegraphed for Dr. Anderson, instructing him to inquire into each case in order to advise the Crown which of the prisoners were worth sending for trial. An extraordinary sequence of events during 1867 led to the barrister being retained during the greater part of the year at a professional fee to help the Government in various ways at the Castle. Then the Clerkenwell explosion occurred, and Lord Mayo asked the young advocate to proceed to London in order to investigate matters connected with the Fenian outrage on the spot.

"I came here," says Dr. Anderson with a quiet smile, "with a return ticket and I have not gone back yet. I came to the Irish office, doing work for Lord Mayo in preparation for the coming Session. The Home Office placed at my disposal all their papers. On April 1st, following, the Secretary of State – Mr. Hardy – now Lord Cranbrook – asked me to go to the Home Office to organise a department there – practically to deal with political crime. I had charge in this country of all reports relating to Fenianism and had certain powers of investigation into various matters of that kind.

Fenianism and political crime happily are not always uppermost in this country, and at different times, in intervals of peace, Dr. Anderson had other work to do. He

acted as secretary to Royal and to Departmental Commissions, and sometimes helped the Chief Secretary for Ireland and the Home Secretary; but he was still occupying the position to which he was originally called, and when disturbed times came he revived the duties.

"All this while," he says, "I was anxious to get back to my profession, but every time there was an opening something intervened. Then I raised distinctly the question that I had no position in the Civil Service, and the Home Secretary offered me

Dr. Robert Anderson

as a temporary arrangement the Secretaryship of the Prison Commission on the passing of the Prison Act in July, 1877. I was still engaged, however, in matters relating to political crime, and afterwards I had the Secretaryship of the Loss of Life at Sea Commission.

"Your duties brought your name before the Parnell Commission?"

"You mean with reference to Le Carron. [*sic*] He was introduced to me in the beginning of 1868, a couple of months after I came to London, and he corresponded with me until he was blown upon by coming up as a witness. I saw a good deal of Mr. Monro, then Assistant Commissioner and my predecessor here, in 1887 and 1888, because of my part in this political crime business, but I was in no way connected with the Metropolitan Police until September 1st, 1888, when I took charge of the "C.I.D.," as we call my department, as Assistant Commissioner, first under Sir Charles Warren and then under Mr. Monro and Sir Edward Bradford, who in turn succeeded to the Commissionership."

And now, having seen Dr. Anderson at home, we will take a peep at him at work.

At the top of the flight of granite steps leading from the principal entrance to the ground floor of New Scotland Yard, a police constable directs the visitor to a little waiting room, whilst an attendant takes his name to Dr. Anderson. In a moment or two we are ushered into a comfortable room, close at hand, on the left of the corridor. It is here, in his official sanctum, that we find the head of that complex organisation known as the Criminal Investigation Department of the Metropolitan Police. Dr. Anderson is an Assistant Commissioner, and his staff – a strong body of picked officers – are concerned with every matter relating to the prevention and detection of crime. These detectives are engaged, it may be, not merely in elucidating mysteries or in making arrests, but in the performance of a large amount of inquiry work, both for the metropolitan and for the provincial and foreign police; and in all their movements they are responsible to their chief, whose controlling hand and inspiring brain govern the conduct of every investigation requiring delicacy and originality of handling.

"I sometimes think myself an unfortunate man," observes the C.I.D. chief, "for between twelve and one on the morning of the day I took up my position here the first Whitechapel murder occurred."

The mention of this appalling sequence of still undiscovered crimes leads to the production of certain ghastly photographs.

"There," says the Assistant Commissioner, "there is my answer to people who come with fads and theories about these murders. It is impossible to believe they were acts of a sane man – they were those of a maniac revelling in blood."

An observation of ours, that in England the police are necessarily hampered a great deal by the freedom-loving characteristics of the people which are opposed to the introduction of measures such as are at the command of the continental police, induces Dr. Anderson to observe that his department has "a great thirst for information," and the public might often assist him very materially by communicating with him in confidence, for very often a small matter sets his officers in motion.

Then Dr. Anderson and his visitor chatted of other things. "Come," said he, "let me show you our new Museum and the Album Room."

So we quitted the cosy apartment, the chief having first spoken through the telephone to Mr. Neame. These telephones and speaking tubes, by the way, give quite an impressive air to the bureau, which, in other respects, with its nicely padded "confessional" chairs, as they might be called, reminds one of a fashionable solicitor's private consultation room, where fair clients confess their sins before seeking divorce. It is betraying no official secret to say that new Scotland Yard is equipped electrically from basement to roof.

From the corridor open various rooms assigned to the department, and a flight of stone steps conducts us to another floor, where Mr. Neame is ready to receive us. First we take a peep into the Museum, which, for the first time in its history, is properly accommodated, arranged, and catalogued. The artist gives a peep of this apartment. A chamber of horrors in its way it nevertheless serves a useful purpose, and it is not maintained to gratify mere curiosity.

Without enumerating its grim contents, or pausing to examine in detail these relics of notorious crimes, one glass case – a new addition – may be mentioned by us. It contains all the implements required for the manufacture of base coin, and a heap of bad silver defies the closest detection. To us the ring, colour, appearance, and even weight of these pewter shillings and half crowns seemed genuine, and in comparing *bona-fide* money with the false there was considerable danger of getting hopelessly mixed. Florins and four-shilling pieces are not so often imitated, the latter being usually examined closely by the public to see if they are not crown pieces.

In a strong room adjoining we are shown watches in great variety and jewellery which has either been taken from prisoners upon arrest or has been "stopped" at the pawnbrokers. A brooch pin of magnificent coloured diamonds, worth at least £100, the experts say, still awaits an owner. It was offered in pawn by a man who, when inquiry was made of him, left the shop and never returned.

"It is extraordinary how often it happens that very unique and costly things – easily to be identified – come into our hands and nobody asks one question about them," observed Dr. Anderson.

Next we take a glance at the rooms full of racks, stored with the portable property of prisoners; all duly ticketed, ready for restoration to their owners, who are usually very particular to have their pound of flesh returned to them when released from gaol.

Then we pass to a room in which a number of police officers in uniform and in ordinary dress are examining photograph albums.

"Looking for your pets?" says Dr. Anderson cheerily.

Under the new system, as the chief explains, these photographs, which now number nearly 50,000, and show in each case the full face, profile, and both hands of the prisoner – are classified according to complexion, age, and height. The facility of ready reference is therefore much increased, a very important consideration when an officer, in the hope of identifying a prisoner as a previous offender, searches through these photographic records to find his likeness.

These albums are always used in combination with an elaborate system of registering habitual criminals. On one page of a book we find the particulars of men who incautiously have tattooed themselves. A common fancy is to imprint upon the body indelibly the words "In memory of," or, what is more frequent still, "I love Mary R -," and so on.

"A man who intends to commit crime ought not to tattoo himself," drily remarks our companion.

A little light upon the objects of all this classification and care is thrown by the remark of Dr. Anderson. "Where a man is twice convicted of crime, the second time on indictment, he becomes liable for seven years after his second sentence to a certain modified police supervision. In order to bring that into operation I have been doing in an extensive and systematic way what was always done in this department to some extent, by getting the photographs of such prisoners and by registering cases which are clearly within the seventh section of the Prevention of Crimes Act."

There is no vindictive spirit in him, for Dr. Anderson finds the pleasant part of his work in helping repentant criminals to reform.

As we take our leave – and by this time we have returned to Dr. Anderson's own room – the Assistant Commissioner sits down to a pile of large sheets. They are the metropolitan criminal returns of the day, giving particulars of every case during the previous twenty-four hours. Curiously enough a spell of bad weather had decreased crime, entailing more poverty and less drunkenness, which is one cause of crime; and bringing discomfort upon the burglary profession, who had therefore remained at home at their ease.

The New York Affair
Part Three
By Wolf Vanderlinden

*Canadian author and researcher **Wolf Vanderlinden** has contributed many articles to these pages over the years, including "The Art of Murder," "Screams of Murder" and the first two parts of this series.*

Carrie Brown

An artist's rendition from
*Jack the Ripper in New York;
or, Piping a Terrible Mystery*
by W.B. Lawson, 1891

INTRODUCTION

On the night of the 23rd of April, 1891, a sixty year old part time prostitute named Carrie Brown, called "Shakespeare" by her friends, entered an East Side New York City flop house, named the East River Hotel, with a client. The hotel register listed them as "C. Kniclo and wife." The next day Brown's body was discovered lying in her room by a hotel employee. She had been struck or punched in the head, strangled, and then the lower part of her body had been horribly mutilated. "C. Kniclo" was nowhere to be found.

The murder suggested to the New York press that London's Jack the Ripper had arrived on American shores. It was pointed out that the chief of the New York Detective Bureau, Chief Inspector Thomas Byrnes, had boasted of the New York police's superiority over their British cousins at Scotland Yard. Jack the Ripper wouldn't last long in New York, Byrnes had crowed, and the question on everyone's mind was: Had the Whitechapel murderer come to test the truth of that assertion?

After an investigation that had lasted only one week, the New York Police arrested and charged an Algerian immigrant named Ameer Ben Ali for the murder. However, given the circumstances of the investigation and the pressure that the police were under to solve the murder quickly, the question still remains: was he responsible for her death? And, if not he, then who? Several possible suspects have been put forth over the years and we will now, in this final part of a three part article, look at some of those suspected to attempt to gauge the likelihood of their guilt. Constraints of space preclude a close look at all suspects, but some will receive a longer look than others depending on their relevance, or perceived relevance, to the case. They are presented in no particular order.

THE SUSPECTS

"The police continue to bring in suspects in the Water street murder case, but there is nothing new to indicate they have captured the right man."

The *Brooklyn Eagle*
29 April, 1891

AMEER BEN ALI

a.k.a.: Frenchy, Frenchy No.1, George Frank, George Francis, George François, Frank Sherlie, Frank Cherlic.

Ameer Ben Ali was born in Algeria and has been described by Edwin M. Borchard, writing in 1932, as being, "an Algerian Frenchman," which, like most of what Borchard has to tell us, is misleading. Instead Ben Ali was a native Algerian Arab and a Muslim. A contemporary report made this clear, stating that he was a "typical Algerian Arab, with a dark, sallow skin, coal-black hair and eyes, and a thin, aquiline nose."[1] Arthur MacDonald offers a less flattering description taken from official sources: "[Ben Ali] *is very large, although stooped, he is more than* [six feet] *in height* [2] *...the cheekbones are extremely prominent, he has small half closed ferret-like eyes and the low face, the yellow skin and the thick jaw do not make the overall effect to be one of intelligence....*[He] *has long and muscular*

Image from *Jack the Ripper; or The Whitechapel Fiend in America,* 1889

arms; he has tattoos in blue ink .... his hands resemble the claws of a bird and he has large feet..."[3]

His complete story is not known but he was able to flesh out some of his history during testimony at his trial and also in various newspaper interviews. Ben Ali, who did not know his own age (Macdonald's official sources could only state that he looked like he was in his forties[4]) was born of the tribe of Ben Asha, or Beni-Aïcha, near the city of Algiers, probably in the town of Ben Aishas. He had been a soldier for eight years serving in the *"first regiment of the Turcos,"*[5] one of the Algerian Zouave regiments that had fought so gallantly for France during the Franco Prussian war of 1870.[6] His regiment was stationed in Algiers and he stated that he had been twice wounded in the leg during the battle of Tizi-Ouzo, in 1870, against the Kabylie,[7] and was removed to hospital where he recuperated for six months. Afterwards he returned to duty and fought another battle against this same tribe. He claims to have been honourably discharged after which he got married in the town of Ben Aishas, had several children and made his living as a common labourer and as a sailor aboard fruit boats that sailed between North Africa and Brasil.

At some point, it becomes apparent that Ben Ali went looking for a better life. He was told, possibly by steamship agents, that he could make a lot of money in the Americas, so in 1888, or 89, he left his home in Algeria and traveled first to Tunis, then to the French port of Marseille where he paid $50 for passage to the northern Brazilian State of Pará.

Brazil turned out to be a mistake. He spoke Arabic as well as some French but this didn't help him in Portugese-speaking Brazil. Worse, he couldn't find a steady job and couldn't make any money. He was finally able to make his way to New York,

however, by working his passage on a Brazilian fruit boat.

Once in New York he found a group of his countrymen and fell in with them living at 379 Fourth Street, Brooklyn. The dream of making his fortune quickly faded and Ben Ali claimed to have been only able to make ends meet by doing odd jobs as a dock labourer and by financial help from his friends. The New York Police, however, scoffed at this and claimed that he actually made his money by begging, sometimes with the aid of a set of splints that enabled him to simulate a broken arm,[8] and by robbing and mistreating the prostitutes of the Fourth Ward, especially those who frequented the East River Hotel from which, it was claimed, he had been ejected at least a half a dozen times.

After roughly eighteen months in New York he had had enough and decided to return to his native land as soon as he could raise the money for passage. Unfortunately for him circumstances would dictate that he would have to put his travel plans on hold for the next eleven years.

As we have seen, the name "Frenchy" came up very early in the police investigation and it is apparent that the police initially had strong suspicion against Ben Ali. The fact that he had been in the company of the murdered woman as well as having spent the night of the murder in the same hotel seemed to make it an open and shut case. Moreover the Algerian's antecedents also served to point the finger at him.

It was proven at the time of Ben Ali's trial that the Algerian was not exactly what one might consider an upright citizen. Indeed part of his year and a half in America was spent as a guest of the penal system. The Algerian himself admitted to having been arrested at least four separate times although he claimed not to have known why. He had spent thirty days in the Jamaica jail in Long Island for reasons that had eluded him. He was also arrested at least once for vagrancy and served thirty days in the Queens County Jail under the name George Frank, the name by which he was also charged in the Carrie Brown murder, having been released from there on 11 April. It was also shown that he had been arrested for larceny after stealing $182 worth of property, a watch and some fruit (as well as, apparently, his name) from one George Franke of Brooklyn. This police record was viewed alongside of Ben Ali's constantly changing story.

Following his arrest Ben Ali first claimed that he had not spent the night in the East River Hotel saying that he had slept in Brooklyn. When faced with several eyewitnesses, however, he was forced to admit that he had spent the night in the murder hotel but he claimed that he did not know Carrie Brown nor had he spent any time with her on the night of the 23rd declaring that the witnesses were all lying. He claimed that he had been in Castle Garden Park on that Thursday night before going over to the hotel at about 11:00 pm. He was given a room which he occupied by himself and which he left at about 5:00 am Friday morning. Far from going into hiding he had instead gone for a walk along the waterfront and had been looking for work.

There was one part of "Frenchy's" story that had no easy explanation: the blood that was supposedly found on him.

Ben Ali claimed that he had worked in a hotel in the town of Jamaica, Long Island, and that he had got the blood on him there after an argument with a woman on the night of the murder. If the woman could be found, the Algerian stated, she would corroborate his story. Detective Aloncle, from the Detective Bureau, had attempted to find the hotel that "Frenchy" was supposed to have worked in but to no avail. He then took Ben Ali with him to Jamaica in order that the prisoner might actually show him

Ameer Ben Ali
from *The New York World*

the hotel but Ben Ali had to admit that it had all been a lie. Later, in an interview with a reporter from the *Brooklyn Daily Eagle,* he changed this story and claimed that he and an unknown man had had a fight in which both were cut. Still later he returned to his original story and claimed that he had had a fight with a woman on the night of the murder but now claimed that the fight had taken place in a basement somewhere in New York, the location of which was unknown to him. It seems that "Frenchy" was the perfect patsy to take the fall for the murder of Carrie Brown.

With a suspect finally charged with the murder on the 30th of April the Coroner wanted to begin the inquest immediately but was forced to postpone the proceedings until 11th of May at the request of Inspector Byrnes and Deputy Assistant District Attorney Lindsay. This would be subsequently pushed back another two days when one of the defence lawyers became ill.

Ben Ali was taken down to the Court of General Sessions late in the afternoon of the

30th and stood before Judge Martine. He gave his name as "George Frank" and, with the help of an interpreter, professed his innocence in a long and rambling monologue. Because he had no money, counsel was provided for him in the form of Levy, Friend & House, Attorneys at Law.[9] Judge Martine then committed Ben Ali to the custody of Inspector Byrnes till the start of the inquest and he was sent back to Police Headquarters in the charge of Capt. McLaughlin. The next day, the 1st of May, 1891, he was removed to New York's Tombs Prison to await his fate.

Viewed today, the grounds for Ben Ali's arrest and indictment were so thin as to be transparent. He was not accused of being "C. Kniclo" but rather it was alleged that he had murdered Carrie Brown after "Kniclo" had left in order to steal her meagre earnings. Various "facts" were used to prove this theory.

Mary Healey

from *The New York World*

It was claimed by the police that Frenchy had such a brutal reputation in the district that the prostitutes of Water Street were afraid of him and would have nothing to do with him. More beast than man he was a violent maniac to be shunned and avoided. The fact that both Mary Healey and Mary Ann Lopez had been in his company the day of the murder was ignored. This fear of the Algerian was not supposed to have affected Carrie Brown, however. She was said to have known Ben Ali intimately and to have been his close friend and, because of this, he was known as *"Shakespeare's mash."* In contrast to this the police also claimed that Ben Ali had threatened to kill Brown only days before her actual murder. There is no real evidence for any of this and certainly none of her friends mentioned any connection between Brown and Ben Ali. The police, on the other hand, needed to connect the two, victim and suspect, in the eyes of the public.

More important was the physical evidence that was supposed to have been discovered at the scene of the murder. The police claimed that on closer examination, a trail of blood was found to lead from Brown's room to Frenchy's. Blood was supposedly found on both sides of his door, on a chair and on the mattress and blanket in his room. Blood was also found on his socks and shirt. Inspector Byrnes claimed that there was a blood spot on the sleeve and also one on the lower part of the front of the shirt that might have occurred when, as he put it, Ben Ali stood or leaned over his victim. The Inspector also claimed that *"There was the mark of a bloody hand on the back of the shirt near the neck that might have been made by the grasp of the woman in her death struggle."*[10] The Inspector would never explain why no one ever heard this death struggle in a hotel with walls little better than boards and a couple occupying the very next room, nor how this evidence, if it was real, contradicted the medical experts who believed that Brown was either dead or unconscious before the mutilations occurred. Finally, blood was also supposed to have been found under Ben Ali's fingernails.

All this blood evidence was chiselled from the floor, scraped from underneath the fingernails and cut from Ben Ali's clothing and sent to a New York City Board of Health doctor, Dr Cyrus Edson. Edson and his colleague, Dr Austin Flint, examined the samples and the newspapers made the claim that *"the blood on the wood was human, and there were traces of the same character under the fingernails"*[11]

Coroner Schultze finally opened the inquest into the death of Carrie Brown on Wednesday the 13th of May. In attendance was the prisoner, Ameer Ben Ali, and all the witnesses who had been locked up in the House of Detention, many since the 24th of April, a period of almost three weeks, during which they were under the constant control of the police.

The first real witnesses of any import were the police, starting with Captain Richard O'Connor of the Oak Street Station. He described the appearance of the body as he first saw it as well as identifying the knife found in the room. The Captain then explained to the inquest how he and his men discovered the trail of blood leading from "Shakespeare's" room to room No. 33 where it was claimed Frenchy had slept. A search also disclosed blood on the bed and other parts of the room. The next witness, Detective Sergeant Crowley, corroborated this and added that the blood had been cut from the floor boards and other woodwork that same day, Friday the 24th, so that it could be sent for analysis.

It is with the next witness that the proceedings take on an air of the "Keystone Cops." Detective Griffin started off innocently enough, corroborating the testimony of O'Connor and Crowley, and stating that he had seen the trail of blood leading from the murder room to Frenchy's. He diverged from the previous witnesses, however, when he claimed that he had seen the trail on Saturday the 25th, a day after it had supposedly been chiselled from the floor!

We can only guess at what his police superiors thought of this fumbling of the evidentiary ball but perhaps they heaved a small sigh of relief when Griffin was offered a second opportunity to get his story straight. The Detective, however, again insisted that he had seen the bloody trail still in situ at a time when the Court had been told it was sitting in Dr. Edson's lab. One can only imagine the full and frank discussion regarding his performance that Detective Griffin was subjected to from his Precinct Captain and the Chief Inspector of Detectives.

It is not this witness, however, who brings the police's blood evidence into doubt. It is the total lack of evidence that it ever existed in the first place. Newspaper reporters who had tramped all over the fifth floor had not seen any of the blood spots either in a trail between the two rooms or scattered around room 33 nor was the blood pointed out to them. Of the trail of blood they wrote incredulously, *"But if any such marks existed they escaped the attention of the reporters who had come in upon the scene while the murdered woman yet lay where she fell, and to do that they must have been very faint indeed."*[12]

After the removal of the body on Friday evening the police left the crime scene without even bothering to lock the door. No guards were posted on rooms 31 and 33, the fifth floor was not made off limits and, as of a day later, the hotel was doing a brisk business, proving the axiom that there is no such thing as bad publicity, selling out all of its rooms with only the exception of No. 31. This room was kept as it was, open for the curious and the morbid to gawk at. According to a reporter from the *World* the blood stained mattress and bedding were still strewn about and one of Carrie Brown's shoes was still propping open a window. Tellingly, neither this reporter, nor any other, made any mention of a series of fresh gouge marks in the floor boards where the police had supposedly chiselled out their trail of blood.

Even if the blood, or evidence of its

removal, was missed by the press it is still difficult to explain the subsequent course of the police investigation. If indeed Ameer Ben Ali had spent the night in room No. 33, or at least if the police believed that he had, and they actually had found a trail of blood connecting the murder room with his, then why didn't they immediately charge the Algerian with the murder? If they were waiting for the report to come back from Dr. Edson before they made the arrest then why did Byrnes elicit the help of the Brooklyn Police; announce that "Frenchy 2" was the killer; employ a drag-net on the 27th, and arrest several men as suspects, or contact the Washington Police on the 28th and advise them to keep a look out for the murderer?

The fact that no non-police witness had seen any trace of the blood trail or blood in room 33, coupled with a story which the police couldn't seem to keep straight, and added to the investigative standstill they found themselves in even a day before the announcement that Frenchy was being charged with the murder, strongly points to the conclusion that the blood evidence was manufactured.

After Deputy Coroner Jenkins had taken the stand and stated that death had been caused by asphyxiation the inquest broke for lunch.

When the inquest reconvened, the jury was subjected to another round of "now you see it, now you don't" with the blood evidence. Eddie Fitzgerald, the night room clerk at the east River Hotel, told how Frenchy obtained a room at around midnight, the night of the murder. He then related how he next saw the prisoner at about 5:00 a.m. when he saw him *"sneak out"* in a suspicious manner. *"'Frenchy'*

> **"At first I refused point blank, much as I liked Byrnes personally, to handle it. The evidence was very flimsy..."**
>
> – *Francis L. Wellman*

kept close to the partition between the barroom and the 'box,' and went out the furthest door, as if to avoid meeting anyone," said the *New York Times*.[13] The inference was clear: Frenchy was acting in a strange manner. Curious, if he was not guilty. Forgotten in all this, however, was the blood evidence that actually had been found and seen by reporters — the blood on the scuttle leading to the roof.

The original police theory, that the murderer had escaped from the roof of the hotel, was now discarded perhaps because it seemed to point more to "C. Kniclo," whom no one saw actually leave the hotel, then Ben Ali, whom Fitzgerald had.

The final witness of the day was Dr. Edson who testified that the various samples sent to him by the police had all turned out to be blood. He would not, indeed could not, proclaim them to be human blood but he did state that he believed them to be human.

The second day, and last of the inquest, started with the jury, the Coroner, Ben Ali and the lawyers visiting the scene of the crime before returning to the Coroner's Court.

The proceedings were then taken up with various witnesses who detailed Carrie Brown's last movements and testified that Frenchy and Brown had been together on the night of the murder and that Frenchy was of a bad character who carried a knife much like the one found in the murder room.

The jury then took only fifteen minutes to decide that there was enough evidence to point to Ameer Ben Ali's guilt. Coroner Schultze then committed the prisoner to the Tombs for the action of the Grand Jury. A crowd of five hundred was said to have hooted and jeered at him as he was led from the building.

On Monday the 18th of May Ben Ali, under the name George Frank, was indicted by the Grand Jury and was sentenced to stand trial for the murder of Carrie Brown.

The trial of Ameer Ben Ali, which took place in Part II of the Court of General Sessions in front of Recorder Frederick Smyth, began on Wednesday the 24th of June, 1891, exactly two months to the day after the death of "Shakespeare." House, Friend & Levy returned for the defendant while Assistant District Attorneys Francis L. Wellman and Charles Simms represented the people. Chief Inspector Byrnes and four of his officers represented the Police.

In his error filled chapter on the Ben Ali trial found in his book *Luck and Opportunity*, Francis L. Wellman, writing almost fifty years after the fact, reports how he supposedly came to the case. *"Whenever Byrnes had some pet case he wanted tried he always wished it on to me. Naturally, therefor, the 'Frenchy' case fell to my lot. At first I refused point blank, much as I liked Byrnes personally, to handle it. The evidence was very flimsy; in their ardor to help their chief make good his boast, the police might very well have mistaken for human blood ordinary stains on the walls of a lodging house of this character.*14

"Byrnes was much upset by my refusal and criticism of his 'evidence.'"

Wellman changed his mind, he claimed, after taking the matter into his own hands and sending the blood evidence to an expert in Philadelphia. A detailed report on this evidence soon arrived, of which Wellman wrote, *"the samples were undoubtably human blood, and second, that the parings of the finger-nails contained particles of partially digested food which could not possibly have been obtained in any other way than during an operation on somebody's smaller intestine."* Wellman

was thus convinced of Ben Ali's guilt and agreed to try the case.

The very nature of the murder and the charge and evidence against Ben Ali caused a problem from the start. So many potential jurymen had read of the crime and had already formed opinions on Ben Ali's guilt or innocence. Some had compunctions against trying a man in a capital case based solely on circumstantial evidence, while others were against the death penalty altogether. It eventually took the first three days just to empanel the twelve jurors needed. Once this was finally accomplished the week was over and the trial was forced to break for the weekend.

The trial didn't really start, therefore, till Day 4, Monday the 29th of June, when the prosecution outlined its case. Assistant District Attorney Wellman spoke for the State. He told of the circumstances of the finding of the body and how Ameer Ben Ali had not only known the victim but had been seen in her company on the night of the murder. Expert testimony, he continued, would show that the blood found upon Ben Ali was identical with the victim's blood found in Room 31.

Wellman also admitted that the man, "C. Kniclo," who had actually rented the room with Carrie Brown was *"unknown to the prosecution"* and unimportant.

The parade of witnesses then began with Mary Corcoran, or Cochrane, the housekeeper at the East River Hotel who had little to offer in the way of evidence. She did, however, admit that she didn't know "Frenchy," an interesting admission if he was as well known in the hotel as the police and prosecution claimed he was. The day ended with Captain O'Connor repeating his testimony, given before the Coroner, of the finding of the body and the blood trail between rooms 31 and 33.

Day 5 of the trial was taken up with several witnesses who gave evidence as to

Ben Ali's character and his movements on the night of the murder. Evidence was brought forward to show that Ben Ali had owned a knife very similar to the one found in room 31. This according to two men, David Galloway and Edward Smith, who had served time in the Queens County Jail with Ben Ali in March and April of that year after the Algerian had been convicted on a vagrancy charge.

Mary Miniter and Eddie Fitzgerald both gave testimony on the events of the 23rd of April and both contradicted statements that they had made earlier to the press when they had not been under the control of the police.

Deputy Corner Jenkins described the wounds to the body and offered that the cause of death was strangulation with the mutilations *"probably"* made after death.

Detective Aloncle, a Francophone officer who was able to converse with Ben Ali, then took the stand to describe various conflicting statements that Ben Ali had made to him regarding how the blood had got on his clothes.

Aloncle was followed by Alice Sullivan who gave evidence regarding the two times that she met up with "Shakespeare" during the day of the murder and described how the second time, at 8:30 at night, Brown had been with "Frenchy."

Day 6 of the trial began with a parade of police witnesses including Chief Inspector Byrnes who gave evidence on the investigation of the murder. They were followed by the medical witnesses.

It rapidly becomes apparent that the evidence offered at the trial closely followed that of the inquest. One exception was the inclusion of two extra medical witnesses. The medical testimony was deemed so important to the conviction of Ben Ali, as indeed it was, that District Attorney DeLancey Nicoll himself rose to examine the three doctors. Although all the evidence

against the Algerian was circumstantial the entire case hinged upon the blood evidence.

Along with Dr. Edson the prosecution added Edson's colleague at the Board of Health, Dr. Austin Flint, as well as an out-of-state heavy hitter, Professor Henry N. Formand, a forensic specialist from the University of Pennsylvania in Philadelphia.

Professor Formand, who claimed to have assisted at or directed some 14,000 post mortem examinations[15] testified that all three had made *"...microscopic, stereoscopic, and chemical examinations of the blood spots upon the mattress upon which the murdered woman lay...."*[16] They discovered that all but six of the blood samples had come from Carrie Brown's abdominal injuries and that *"intestinal matter mingled with blood of Carrie Brown was identical with that found upon 'Frenchy,' upon his clothing and in the room where he slept"* and that *"the intestinal matter found in the various places were identical."*[17] Professor Formand declared he was *"willing to stake his life upon the fact"* but was forced to admit that he couldn't swear if the blood was human or not. Both Drs. Edson and Flint agreed with their esteemed colleague.

Disregarding the possibility that the police found some other donor, it is safe to assume that all the blood sent to Drs. Formand, Edson, and Flint was indeed from Carrie Brown and the murder room and would thus contain the same characteristics. This is especially true of the bloody trail which may have been tracked from one room to the next by any number of people including police, reporters or any of the curious throng who were allowed to freely visit the crime scene.

With the medical testimony concluded, the prosecution closed the case for the people.

Abraham Levy rose and motioned that with no testimony as to the whereabouts of the man who accompanied Carrie Brown to

Carrie Brown

Photo courtesy New York City Municipal Archives

the East River Hotel on the night of her murder, his client could not be found guilty and so the case should be thrown out. His motion was denied, however, and the court adjourned for the day.

On the seventh day of the trial the defence presented its case. The first witness was Constable James R. Hiland, the man who had arrested Ben Ali on the vagrancy charge in Queens, who testified that he had searched the prisoner most carefully and that Ben Ali had no knife on him when he was arrested. Galloway and Smith's damaging testimony that linked the Algerian with the murder weapon was thus demolished.

In what later proved to be a monumental mistake by the defence, the defendant, Ameer Ben Ali, next took the stand. He proved to be a poor witness and it was afterwards commented that the translator, a cigar merchant working out of the Hotel Metropole named Emil Sultan, had unquestionably earned his money that day.

Things started slowly with Ben Ali calmly giving his life story but the Algerian's cool demeanor was only an illusion. When asked outright, *"Did you kill Carrie Brown?"* he changed instantly. Losing all restraint, he seemed to explode from his chair as he leapt up and began wildly gesticulating with his hands and arms. Sometimes weeping, he asserted his complete innocence. He didn't know the victim, he claimed. He didn't kill her, he didn't kill anyone. The knife wasn't his, and he had never seen it before.

Upon cross-examination by Assistant District Attorney Wellman he was erratic and unconvincing in his answers. The witnesses who had testified to seeing him with Brown on the night of the murder were brought into the court and he was asked if he knew them. He said he only recognized Mary Ann Lopez. Wellman pointed out Alice Sullivan who had testified in court

that she had seen "Shakespeare" with Ben Ali that night. Ben Ali looked at her for a brief moment then jumping to his feet, his finger wildly stabbing the air in her direction, exclaimed, *"Do you know me? Have I ever seen you?"*

Asked to explain his police record he claimed that he had been arrested four times but had absolutely no idea why.

Asked how the blood had got on his clothes he responded that he had got it on himself while he was in a basement. *"In the name of God, I cannot tell what basement,"* he replied when pressed as to its location.

When it was pointed out to him that Detective Aloncle had testified that Ben Ali had told him in French that he got the blood on him somewhere in Jamaica, he cried out *"He don't tell the truth by Allah!"*

A.D.A. Wellman's relentless questioning finally caused Ben Ali to once more jump to his feet and exclaim in frustration, *"If they want to kill me they can."* Ben Ali was then allowed to leave the witness stand.

All in all a very bad impression was made on the jury. Professor Formand, the blood expert, went so far as to suggest that the medical testimony was not the most important factor in obtaining Ben Ali's conviction, but that, *"In his own opinion the placing of the Algerian on the stand in his own behalf was sufficient to bring about his own conviction..."*[18] If Wellman can be believed, he deliberately pursued a strategy of attacking and enraging Ben Ali purposely so that the jury could see the Algerian in as worse a light as possible. *"Nobody, of course could make out what he was saying, but guilty or innocent, it was apparent to everybody that it would not be safe to let such a wild man go free."*[19]

The trial was not yet officially over, however. The defence's own medical experts: Drs. George S. Huidekoper, Paul Gibier, Justin Herald and Prof. Henry A. Mott, next paraded to the stand. They contradicted the testimony given by the State's experts and stated that not all the blood samples had indications that they had come from the intestines and couldn't, therefore, be linked to the murder. Under cross examination, however, they all did have to admit that Dr. Formand was the top man in his field and that each of them respected his opinion.

This concluded the presentation of the defence and, after a little testimony in rebuttal was given by the prosecution, the court adjourned for the day. It was expected that the trial would wrap up with Mr. Frederick B. House speaking for his client and Mr. Wellman for the people.

The eighth and final day of the trial started with a reappearance of Deputy Coroner Jenkins who refuted statements made by one of the defence doctors. With all the evidence presented, the lawyers began their final summation.

Frederick B. House for the defence was the first to speak and, with Ameer Ben Ali beginning to weep, he placed his hands on his clients forehead in a sympathetic manner as if to emphasize the need for humanity in the case. House discussed the evidence at length and pointed out that it was all circumstantial and *"of the most unsatisfactory kind and bearing the least weight."*[20]

He then got to the heart of the whole case against his client, asking the all important question: *"Where is the man who went up stairs in the Fourth Ward hotel with old 'Shakespeare' the last time she was seen alive? When he went up stairs he passed out of sight. No one knows where he went or where he is."*[21] Of course this question could not then be answered by either the police or the prosecution, and it never would be.

> "My friend Tom Byrnes had made good his boasted superiority to Scotland Yard..."
>
> – *Francis L. Wellman*

House next brought up the lack of motive for his client and went over the testimony of the experts, stressing that although they swore as to what food the victim had eaten, they could not swear that the blood they examined was even human. This concluded the defence of Ameer Ben Ali.

In a surprise move, District Attorney Nicoll rose to sum up for the people. He spoke in a calm, cool and even manner, without flowery eloquence or any attempt to elicit passionate feeling. It was not a case for sentiment, he said, the jury was to weigh the evidence without thought of sympathy and to come to a decision based simply upon the facts. He dwelt at some length on the testimony of the experts and pointed out the various contradictory statements the prisoner had made, not only to the detectives but to the court as well. Where Mr. House had seen no motive, D.A. Nicoll was of the opinion that the fact that the pocket in Carrie Brown's dress had been turned inside out clearly showed the intention of robbery, a naive observation when dealing with a mutilation murder with clear psychosexual overtones.

When the District Attorney had finished, it was time for Recorder Smyth to charge the jury. He spoke for an hour and thirty-five minutes, carefully explaining the law of evidence and then condensing the testimony given in the case. His summation seemed to come down squarely on the side of the prosecution as he stated that there was no doubt that the blood was indeed human and had come from the victim. The intestinal matter found in the blood proved this, he claimed. He also pointed out that the medical experts for the prosecution had the benefit of examining the actual blood samples themselves while the experts for the defence, on the other hand, had only the written reports supplied by the prosecution on which to base their findings. It was up to the jury, he said, to decide which testimony was entitled to the greater weight. The jury then filed out.

They deliberated for only two hours, during which time they voted three times. After the first ballot it was 8 to 4 for murder in the first degree. After the second it stood at 11 to 1 also for murder in the first degree but there they had hit a roadblock put up by the lone jury member who refused to budge. After some spirited argument and apparently no hope of changing their colleague's decision, and with the possible loss of their Fourth of July holiday looming, they reached a compromise.

The courtroom was packed and waited in excited anticipation as the jury filed back in with their verdict. *"Guilty,"* the foreman announced, *"guilty of murder in the second degree."* A low murmur of surprise ran through the packed room, more for the degree of the crime than the guilt of the defendant.

Apprised of the verdict by his interpreter, Ameer Ben Ali was left standing in a daze. He had cheated the executioner but wondered what his fate would now be. His relief quickly changed to dismay when he was told that he might face life in jail. *"What can I do?"* was his hopeless exclamation.

Recorder Smyth discharged the jury and remarked that he was free to express the feeling that they had arrived at the correct result. District Attorney Nicoll expressed his satisfaction with the outcome, adding that the jury probably realized that there was a lack of positive proof of premeditation and deliberation in the murder.

Although Chief Inspector Byrnes parroted D.A. Nicoll and said that he was very much pleased with the verdict, it is hard to believe that he was speaking the truth. The police had gone out of their way to have Ameer Ben Ali found guilty. Witnesses had been manipulated, evidence had been manufactured and one member of the jury had claimed to the press that certain jury members had been bought. The result of this was not the resounding affirmation of his own and his department's abilities that he had expected. Although Ben Ali had been found guilty, he had not been proved to have been the dangerous premeditated killer that Byrnes had hoped the world would see him as.

There is at least one indication that the Ripper was not far from his thoughts. When a reporter asked him if he thought that Ben Ali was Jack the Ripper, Byrnes replied that he would not like to express an opinion on that subject, but went on to claim that he had in his possession a written statement which proved that the guilty man had been in London at the times of the Whitechapel murders. Needless to say, no one actually saw this statement or was able to prove that it ever existed, however it does tend to show what message Chief Inspector Byrnes was trying to get across to the world. Assistant District Attorney Wellman later offered an even clearer view of Byrnes' motives, saying, *"My friend Tom Byrnes had made good his boasted superiority to Scotland Yard, of which, by the way, he was always very Jealous."*[22]

On 10 July, 1891, Ameer Ben Ali was sentenced to prison for life to be served at Sing Sing, the New York State prison. On 21 January, 1893, he was transferred to the State Hospital for Insane Criminals at Dannemora until he was pardoned on 16 April 1902. He returned to New York for just one day before sailing on the French ship *La Touraine* first to France and then back to his native Algeria.

Did Ameer Ben Ali murder Carrie Brown? The answer has got to be the Scottish verdict of not proven. He was seen with Brown on the night of the murder, although he denied it, but it should be noted that the two were part of a small group, and Ben Ali was coupled with Mary Anne Lopez that night, not Carrie Brown.

After first being caught in a lie Ben Ali finally did admit that he spent the night in the East River Hotel on the evening of the 23/24 of April and he did apparently have blood on him when arrested. There was no real evidence that he had spent the night in room No. 33 however, and no credible proof that the blood on his person actually came from "Shakespeare."

Although his character was proved to be unsavoury and testimony was offered that he abused and robbed the women of the Fourth Ward, there was no real proof that he had even owned a knife at the time of the murder, let alone ever used one against anyone.23

The police investigation into the crime was mishandled and its findings were dubious to say the least. The blood evidence against him was so suspect as to be worthless and indeed its value, or lack thereof, was one of the main reasons that Ben Ali was later pardoned. The inescapable conclusion that the police manufactured evidence should on its own point to a lack of real evidence, other than the merest circumstantial kind, linking the Algerian with the murder. Add to this the fact that the police never were able to track down "C. Kniclo" and the case against Ben Ali crumbles into dust.

After the trial the editor of the *New York Times* questioned "Frenchy's" guilty verdict and the police's hand in it. Summing up the situation in a nutshell he stated:

"The head of our detective force is un-doubtably a keen and energetic officer, but he has more than once shown that success in catching and convicting somebody is more to him then the demands of exact justice. Even such a wretched specimen as *this Algerian ought not to be sacrificed on insufficient evidence merely to demonstrate the infallibility of our detective system."*24

CHARLES HOLLAND

On May 1st, 1891, a piano tuner named Charles Holland, aged 40, was arrested in the village of Jamaica, Long Island. Constable Ashmead, the arresting officer, originally detained Holland merely because he resembled the description of the murderer of Carrie Brown, but he was locked up in the jail cells in the town hall when it was discovered that he had in his pocket two heavily bloodstained handkerchiefs.

When questioned, Holland stated that he was married with four children. His home was in the village of Rye in Westchester County, New York, but his wife had thrown him out. He freely admitted that he was in New York on the night of the murder but said that he had lodged at the New England Hotel in the Bowery and was nowhere near the East River Hotel. New York police were notified of the arrest but declined to make any effort to determine whether Holland was "C. Kniclo" or not, as Ameer Ben Ali had already been charged with the murder.

Holland did not fade quickly into the background, however, since the Long Island police and Ameer Ben Ali's defence team maintained an interest in him, especially when it was proved that parts of his story were false. Holland gave conflicting versions of how the blood had got on the handkerchiefs, and it was proved that on the night of the murder the New England Hotel had been closed for repairs.

Investigations in Rye seemed to indicate that Holland was a mild mannered individual who never quarrelled with his wife but who did have a bit of a drinking problem. It was on account of these "sprees" that his wife had turfed him out. His wife, described as a respectable woman, felt that her husband was too much of a coward to have committed any murder, let alone one so bloody and vicious, and this opinion was supported by family and friends who laughed at the idea.

In the end there is absolutely no credible evidence linking Charles Holland with the murder of Carrie Brown, and what little we do know about the man, forty years old and not German, seems to rule him out.

SEVERIN KLOSOWSKI
a.k.a.: George Chapman, Ludwig Zagowski, Ludwig Schloski

The third and perhaps the most important suspect is Severin Klosowski, better known as George Chapman. Important because in one sense the names Carrie Brown and George Chapman have become united in a relationship of mutual consequence, each adding to the name of the other. Had there been no Chapman, Carrie Brown would be largely forgotten now. Had there been no Brown, the case against Chapman as Jack the Ripper would suffer.

Chapman's early years in Poland can be pieced together using documents found by Inspector Godley upon Chapman's arrest on the 25th of October 1902.

George Chapman, the son of a carpenter, was born Severin Klosowski in the Polish town of Nagornak on 15 December, 1865. As a teenager he was apprenticed to a surgeon in order to become a surgical assistant or feldscher. After four and a half years of study he moved to Warsaw and found employment as a surgical assistant. Sometime later he emigrated to Great Britain.

What we do know is that Chapman first appeared in London working as a hairdresser's assistant to Abraham and Ethel Radin at 70 West India Dock Road in Poplar and that Chapman worked for the Radins for roughly five months. What we don't know is when exactly this was. The best that can be said is Chapman probably arrived in London in late1887 or possibly early 1888.

Klosowski is next recorded running his own barber shop at 126 Cable Street, St. George's-in-the-East in 1889. It seems likely that he was living here during the Ripper murders of 1888 and certainly not under the White Hart public house on the corner of Whitechapel High Street and George Yard (steps from where Martha Tabram was found murdered) as R. Michael Gordon claims in his book *Alias Jack the Ripper*.[25] Given his later crimes, the theory goes, it is this presence in Whitechapel during the Ripper murders that makes Chapman a possible suspect.

On the 29th of October, 1889, Klosowski married Lucy Baderski[26] in what was probably a bigamous marriage, as a woman is said to have arrived from Poland claiming to be the rightful Mrs. Klosowski. What eventually happened to this woman is not known except that she apparently left the Chapmans' home where she had been staying.

On the 6th of September, 1890, a son, Wladyslaw, was born to Lucy and Severin, but the boy didn't live to see his first birthday, dying on 3 March, 1891. Sometime soon after the death the Klosowskis moved to Jersey City, New Jersey, in the United States.

This move, coming as it did sometime around the Ripper-like murder of Carrie Brown, is seen by some as evidence of Chapman's possible guilt. Indeed until recently the Polish hairdresser stood as the only Ripper suspect connected to both

Whitechapel in 1888 and New York City in 1891.

Life in the New World turned out to be less than idyllic and the couple soon quarrelled over Severin's womanizing. Disheartened and pregnant, Lucy returned to London in February, 1892, and gave birth to a daughter, Cecilia, in May. Klosowski followed his wife back to London in late May or early June. After an attempted reconciliation the couple went their separate ways.

After a year long relationship with a woman named Sarah Ann Chapman, known as Annie Chapman,[27] Klosowski changed his name to George Chapman and soon after became a publican, owning and running a series of pubs. This was the start of Chapman's career as the "Borough Poisoner" and between the years 1895 and 1902 he met, "married" and then murdered three women by poisoning them with antimony; Mrs. Mary Spink on Christmas Day, 1897, Bessie Taylor on the 13 of February, the day before Valentines Day, 1901 and Maud Marsh on 22 October 1902.

After his arrest in 1902, Severin Klosowski, alias George Chapman, became linked with both the Whitechapel murders and the murder of Carrie Brown through a report in a London newspaper that suggested that the police had made this connection. This theory was given some credence when the *Pall Mall Gazette* interviewed the retired Chief Inspector Frederick Abberline in order to ask his opinion on the subject.

In the interview, which was published on the 24 March, 1903, Abberline stated, *"...there are scores of things which make one believe that Chapman is the man; ...there is a coincidence also in the fact that the murders ceased in London when 'Chapman' went to America, while similar murders began to be perpetrated in America after he landed there."*

Abberline went on to state his belief that the Ripper may have been harvesting organs for the mysterious American doctor who had been mentioned by Coroner Wynne Baxter during the inquest into the death of Annie Chapman. He stated, *"It is a remarkable thing... that after the Whitechapel horrors America should have been the place where a similar kind of murder*

**Severin Klosowski
a.k.a. George Chapman**

from *The Murderer's Who's Who* 1979

began, as though the miscreant had not fully supplied the demand of the American agent."

In a follow-up interview, published on the 31st of March, 1903, Abberline told the *Pall Mall Gazette, "...Seeing that the same kind of murders began in America afterwards, there is much more reason to think the man emigrated."* A trend was thus started which seemed to carry official sanction.

The trend, which continues to this day, really got off the ground when Hargrave Adam wrote *The Trial of George Chapman* for the *Notable British Trials Series* in 1930. Adam was the first to publish in book form the suggestion that Chapman was the Ripper and that Chapman murdered Carrie Brown in New York in 1891. As the years went by several authors have looked at Chapman as a Ripper suspect and have, for the most part, based their theories about his guilt on Chief Inspector Abberline's opinions.

So, does Abberline's argument prove Chapman's guilt? Did Chapman murder Carrie Brown? The short answer to that question is no, he did not, and there are several reasons why.

It should be understood that any consideration for Chapman's guilt in the Brown case depends on a couple of assumptions: that George Chapman was Jack the Ripper and that Carrie Brown was murdered by Jack the Ripper. The second point will be discussed later in this article. On the first point, constraints of space do not allow me to go into any great detail, but I will try to give the most compelling reason why I would disregard Chapman as a viable Ripper suspect.

The man who "marries" women and then slowly poisons them to death in the privacy of his own home when he tires of them does not display the same psychopathology as the man who murders and mutilates women in the streets and courts of a crowded city. It is difficult, if not impossible, to reconcile Chapman's relationship with Bessie Taylor, which lasted for almost three years before he killed her, with the Ripper's modus operandi. Several authors, from George R. Sims to Edmund Pearson to Donald Rumbelow to Paul Begg, have rightly pointed this out as well.

Those who support Chapman's candidacy tend to mention "his cruelty" or "his cunning" or point to other serial killers who changed their murder methodology during their careers but unless these men are of the same specific type of killer, the "ripper, mutilator" as the Whitechapel murderer was, the comparison is faulty. Whatever demons drove Jack the Ripper drove him to cut and mutilate. Chapman seems to have killed for profit or from boredom. John Douglas, ex of the FBI's behavioural science unit, states: *"...there is no way a man hacks apart five or six women, lies low for ten years with no one noticing anything about him, then resumes his homicidal career as a poisoner, who, along with bombers, are the most cowardly and detached of all murderers. It just doesn't happen that way in real life."*[28]

Those who still champion Chapman as the Ripper and thus the killer of Carrie Brown have some other hurdles to overcome, such as the description of the murderer given by Mary Miniter. Miniter described the man thus, *"a man about thirty-two to thirty-five years of age. He was about 5 feet 8 ½ inches tall and slim build. He had a long sharp nose and a heavy blond moustache... I thought the man was German."*

R. Michael Gordon states that this *"was a detailed word picture of Severin Klosowski."* Yes, exactly... except for the fact that Klosowski was younger, shorter, had a medium build, didn't have a long sharp nose, had black hair and was a Pole. Despite some writers' ludicrous attempts to prove otherwise, George Chapman does not match the eyewitness description of "C. Kniclo," the man who murdered Carrie Brown.

Even if one brushes aside the differences in description, Klosowski's guilt or innocence in the Brown murder still hinges on one simple question: was Severin Klosowski in New York City on the night of the 23/24 of April 1891? There is evidence that suggests that he was not.

The British National Census for 1891

shows that Klosowski and his wife, Lucy, were still in London living at 2 Tewkesbury Buildings, Whitechapel, when the census was taken on 5 April. Did he have enough time to sail to New York and commit the murder?

Philip Sugden makes the reasonable suggestion that if Klosowski and his wife had left London soon after the census was taken then there was still time for an Atlantic crossing and an arrival in New York before the 23 of April. Perhaps, Sugden suggests, the death of their son in early March may have been the catalyst for a voyage at that time. This is obviously possible, but no evidence has been found to support it.[29] R. Michael Gordon thinks otherwise.

In his recent book *The American Murders of Jack the Ripper*[30] Mr. Gordon has found what he believes to be proof of Severin Klosowski's arrival in New York City on the 23rd of April, 1891. He found a startling piece of evidence: the New York Passenger Arrivals Lists show that a "Sveri" or "Sverni" (Mr. Gordon was unable to decipher the first name), Koslowsky arrived in the Port of New York aboard the ship *S. S. Waesland* only hours before the murder of Carrie Brown. Mr. Gordon is so sure that this is indeed Severin Klosowski that he states it as fact in his Appendix III writing that *"Klosowski and wife Lucy move to New York City only weeks after the last Ripper murder. Arriving on April 23, 1891."* A closer look finds serious flaws in Mr. Gordon's evidence.

The fact that the name listed is Koslowsky rather than Klosowski is rather meaningless. Mr. Gordon reasonably points out that it could have been written by an official *"...who was surely unfamiliar with Polish names or their spellings."* But the man listed was described as being 30 years old while Klosowski had just recently turned 25. Was this official unfamiliar with Polish ages as well? Also, there is no record of Klosowski's wife Lucy, who was travelling with him and who would have been listed as well. A listing of a Lucy Koslowsky next to "Sveri" or "Sverni" Koslowsky would have been enough evidence to erase most doubt, but she does not appear.

Furthermore there are questions raised by the ship that this Koslowsky sailed on, the *S. S. Waesland*. Mr. Gordon tells us that *"...the S. S. Waesland, which also sailed the Atlantic passenger routes from Belgium to England and then on to New York City during 1891."* This may be true but Gordon offers us no proof that it actually was true. What he does offer us is the Ships Listing from the *New York Times* for the 23rd April, 1891. This reports:

S. S. Waesland (Belg.,) Grant, Antwerp 11ds., with mdse. and passengers to Peter Wright & Sons. Arrived at the bar at 1:50 P.M.

This Ships Listing supplies some interesting information to those who know how to read it. It tells us that the *S. S. Waesland*, of Belgian registry, was captained by a man named Grant. The ship sailed from the Belgian port of Antwerp and **sailed directly to New York,** with the journey taking eleven days. The ship was carrying both merchandise and passengers.

If this ship had stopped in London or anywhere in Britain in order to pick up passengers the ports of call would have been listed after the city of Antwerp. Since no ports other than Antwerp are listed, the voyage was non-stop. It is difficult, therefore, to imagine that Severin Klosowski and his wife would take the time, trouble and money to travel all the way to Belgium in order to take passage to New York when several ships were leaving the Port of London every week for that same destination.

This theorising is unnecessary, however, as the answer to this question has been published by more than one source but never commented on.

Buried in the transcripts of Chapman's trial is the witness statement of Mrs. Stanislaus Rauch, nee Baderski. Mrs. Rauch was the sister of Lucy Baderski, Klosowski's wife at the time of the move to New Jersey. She had given evidence at the Police Court Proceedings on 7th of January, 1903, and would later take the witness stand on the first day of Chapman's trial.

It is from Mrs. Rauch's testimony that we have obtained the information that Chapman and his wife left for America in 1890, a fact that is obviously wrong based on the information provided by the 1891 census. So Mrs. Rauch was wrong on this point but does this mean that we should throw out all of her testimony? If it could be proved that she intentionally mislead the court or was lying or covering up for Chapman for some reason then perhaps her information should be disregarded but there is absolutely no evidence of this and it is highly improbable that she did so.

It seems evident that Mrs. Rauch merely had a little trouble remembering the exact year, much like another witness at the trial, Wolf Levisohn, which is perhaps understandable after the passage of thirteen years. The information that she has provided appears to be correct, but she has simply pushed back the year when these events took place. For example, when she stated at the Police Court Proceedings that she had arrived "from German Poland in August 1889," it was actually a year later, 1890.[31] When she stated at the trial that, "*I remember him and my sister going to America. She came back alone in February, 1891,*" we know that the month is correct but that it was actually a year later, 1892. This mistake was consistent throughout her testimony.

Under cross examination by Chapman's lawyers, Mrs. Rauch was asked: "*Had you seen the accused very often before he went to America?*" To which Mrs. Rauch replied: "*Yes. I came over here in August, and they went to America about the following Whitsuntide.*"[32] As Mrs. Rauch had arrived in London in August of 1890 then "the following Whitsuntide" would have fallen in 1891, the year we know that Chapman and his wife did indeed leave for America.

The religious observance of Whitsun, or Pentecost, is held seven Sundays after Easter in mid Spring. Whitsuntide, also known as Whitsun week, is comprised of Whitsun Sunday and the following week ending on the next Sunday. Mrs. Rauch's evidence can be taken to mean that Chapman and his wife left London for America sometime shortly before or after Whitsun in the year 1891. In that year Whitsun fell on the 17th of May. Therefore, according to his sister-in-law, Severin Klosowski left London around the week of the17th to the 24th of May, 1891, and was thus still in London some three weeks to a month *after* the murder of Carrie Brown and wouldn't even arrive in New York City until either very late May or early to mid June.

If we take this to be true, then Severin Klosowski, alias George Chapman, is definitely innocent of the murder of Carrie Brown.

HENRY G. DOWD
a.k.a.: "Jack the Slasher"

On 17 January, 1892, Henry G. Dowd was arrested in New York for the murder of John Carson and knife attacks on six other men. Dowd had been dubbed "Jack the Slasher" by the press, who also linked him with the Whitechapel murders and the murder of Carrie Brown.

It is obvious why Dowd was linked with the Brown case (although there was absolutely no evidence placing him anywhere near London in 1888), as the assaults took place in the same notorious slum area and within blocks of the East River Hotel where "Jack the Ripper" had already struck.

Today we would point out that all of Dowd's victims including his earlier non lethal, and non slasher, assaults were against men and not women. This shows a very different psychopathology at work. Moreover, even though he chose male victims inebriated to the point of stupefaction he was not skilled enough to actually cause death with the use of his razor. The one victim that he did manage to murder he had found lying unconscious in the street.

Dowd's description also does not match with Mary Miniter's description of the killer. Dowd, who was forty years old in 1891, was described as being *"...probably 5 feet 11 inches in height... has a shambling gait and is slouchy and awkward. He has a red complexion, heavy cheek bones and hollow cheeks, a repulsive mouth that he purses in a decisive fashion when it is not twitched so that the left corner is higher than the other, a furtive eye, gaunt hands, large feet, and dark hair."*[33] Edited down, Dowd was older, taller and had dark hair rather than blond hair. Dowd was also not German.

It is highly unlikely that Henry Dowd had anything to do with the murder of Carrie Brown.

FRANK CASTELLANO

On March 19, 1893, a woman in New York was attacked with a knife. She was *"ripped up the side ... and a big knife was left sticking out of the wound."*[34] By 21 March, Captain Doherty and the men of the Fifth Precinct were able to trace the knife to one Frank Castellano, an Italian barber who had been a fireman aboard a trans-Atlantic steamer.

The New York Police were convinced that Castellano's journeys across the Atlantic, coupled with his supposed knife assault on a woman, were strong evidence that the ex-fireman was in fact Jack the Ripper. His connection with the Lower East Side added suspicion that he had murdered Carrie Brown as well.

I can find no more information about this man other than these basic facts and can only point out that Castellano was not of German origin.

DR. FRANCIS TUMBLETY
(variously spelled as: Tumbleton, Twomblety, Tumilty or Tumuelty)
a.k.a.: Dr. J.H. Blackburn, Frank Townsend, Phillip Sternberg, Mike Sullivan, the Indian Herb Doctor

Dr. Francis Tumblety's consideration for being the murderer of Carrie Brown rests on two points: his candidacy for being Jack the Ripper and the fact that he was living in the United States at the time of the New York murder. But was he actually in New York on the night of "Shakespeare's" death?

Stephen Ryder recently discovered that he was apparently staying at the Plateau Hotel in Hot Springs, Arkansas, when it was reported burgled on the 17th of April, 1891, almost a week before the murder. Tumblety was said to have lost $2,000 dollars in cash and $5,000 worth of diamonds in the robbery. It seems unlikely that he would have had the inclination to leave Arkansas quickly after this loss. The demands of the police investigation alone would have probably kept him in Hot Springs for at least a couple of days, and if he was anxious for the return of his property or at least word of any police progress then it is safe to assume that he would have stayed even longer.

However, if the "doctor" actually had

Dr. Francis Tumblety
from *The Atchison Daily Globe* 1888

left Arkansas soon after the theft he could easily have made it to New York in time to murder Carrie Brown on the night of the 23/24. Nevertheless, there is no indication that he actually did travel to New York from Arkansas, and the eyewitness evidence of Mary Miniter alone would tend to disprove any link between Tumblety and the death of "Shakespeare."

Tumblety was uniquely recognizable

with his height, long walrus mustache and his eccentricity in dress, which was constantly commented upon. One report described him as *"...a very tall, muscular man, of rather handsome and imposing appearance, with a huge black mustache..."*[35] He himself stated that the description on his military pass from 1865 was *"...height, six feet; eyes, blue; complexion, fair; hair, dark..."* His age in 1891 would be roughly 61 years old, and it is known that he still affected the large flowing mustache as late as 1888.

This does not compare favourably with the description of "C. Kniclo," who was much younger (32 to 35), was shorter (5 feet 8 to 5 feet 9), had a thin build, blond hair and a heavy blond mustache and was described as being German. It is apparent that Dr. Francis Tumblety did not enter the East River Hotel with Carrie Brown on the night of the murder and was not her killer.

CARL FERDINAND FEIGENBAUM
a.k.a. Karl Zahn, Anton Zahn

Carl Ferdinand Feigenbaum was executed on 27 April, 1896, for the murder of Mrs. Juliana Hoffman, from whom he rented a room. In what was an apparent robbery attempt Feigenbaum attacked Mrs. Hoffman with a knife while she slept, cutting her throat and stabbing her. Her son, Michael, was able to flee the attacker by climbing out a window. His cries for help summoned the police, and Feigenbaum was quickly arrested.

The execution might have been the end to the matter except that later that same day Feigenbaum's lawyer, William Sanford Lawton, announced to the press that it was his belief that Feigenbaum was actually Jack the Ripper. The lawyer believed that his client had also been responsible for several other murders including the murder of Carrie Brown.

Lawton felt that his client was secretive, crafty, very intelligent, and able to converse on such topics as surgery and dissection. Lawton also pointed out that although Feigenbaum acted as if he were a penniless tramp he actually left his sister property in both Cincinnati and New York. Lawton also claimed that his client had confessed to him that he suffered from a mania to kill and mutilate women and that he had been in Wisconsin, during a series of murders there, and in London in 1888. Lawton also believed that the murder of Mrs. Hoffman was a botched Ripper attack pointing out that there was some old blood on Feigenbaum's knife, possible evidence of some earlier murder. The fact that Feigenbaum seemed to fit the murderer of Carrie Brown, as he was, after all, German and had murdered a woman in New York with a knife, also led Lawton to believe that his client was responsible for the murder of "Shakespeare."

Did Carl Feigenbaum murder Carrie Brown? There is not enough evidence to say either way. It could not be proved that he was even in New York on the night of the 23/24 of April, 1891. The *New York Times* pointed out that the motive for the murder of Mrs. Hoffman seemed to be based solely on robbery. Moreover, although he was German, Feigenbaum was forty nine years old in 1891, much older than the man seen by Mary Miniter. It should also be noted that Feigenbaum never really admitted to anything including the murder of Mrs. Hoffman. No one other than Lawton could claim to have actually heard any confession of homicidal mania from him. Although Lawton stated that he had proof that his client had been in London in 1888, he never produced it.

That Carl Feigenbaum was a cold blooded killer is an established fact, but whether or not he murdered anyone other than Mrs. Hoffman is unproven.

EMIL TOTTERMAN
a.k.a. Carl Nielsen

On Sunday the 20th of December, 1903, the body of prostitute Sarah Martin was found in a second floor room of Kelly's Hotel at the corner of James Slip and Water Street, only two and a half blocks from what had been the East River Hotel. She had been strangled and mutilated. She had gone up to the room with a man who had registered as Carl Nilsen. No one had seen this man leave the building and it was assumed that he had climbed out a window. The newspapers, not surprisingly, connected the death of Sarah Martin with the killing of Carrie Brown and the Jack the Ripper murders.

Once more the Oak Street Station House was called out to deal with a Ripper-like murder in its precinct. The man in charge of the case was "Chesty" George McClusky. McClusky, now an Inspector although he had been Chief of Detectives,[36] was the same officer who almost thirteen years earlier had interviewed Arbie La Bruckman in his Jersey cell and had told the Jersey police to cut him loose.

Through some evidence that had been left at the scene, including a piece of wrapping paper on which was written his real name, a Finnish born sailor named Emil Totterman was quickly arrested.

Totterman was tried and convicted of the murder of Sarah Martin and sentenced to death, but the sentence was commuted because of his heroic war service during the Spanish American War. Totterman was released from prison on Christmas Eve, 1929, and returned to his native Finland.

The similarities between the murder of Carrie Brown and Sarah Martin are interesting: both prostitutes: both murdered in Fourth Ward hotels within blocks of each other, both first strangled then mutilated with a knife, both times the killer escaped unseen from the building. Totterman even had reddish blond hair, and it could be argued that his Finnish nationality could be confused with German. But, as Michael Conlon points out,[37] Totterman was 29 years old at the time of his trial in 1904 and would have thus been only 16 or 17 when Carrie Brown met her fate in 1891 — much too young to have been "Shakespeare's" killer.

The Reverend JOHN GEORGE GIBSON
a.k.a.: Pastor Jack Gibson

In 1999 author Robert Graysmith published the highly entertaining, yet seriously flawed, book *The Bell Tower. The Case of Jack the Ripper Finally Solved...in San*

The Reverend John George Gibson

Originally from *The San Francisco Chronicle*, taken from Graysmith's *The Bell Tower*, 1999

Francisco.[38] The book looks at the famous "Demon in the Belfry"case, the murder of two young women in the Emmanuel Baptist Church in San Francisco in April 1895. Canadian born medical student and Sunday school teacher William Henry Theodore Durrant was found guilty of the crimes and eventually hanged.

Graysmith postulates that Durrant was actually innocent, and he pins the real blame on the church's then minister, the Reverend John George Gibson. This was not a new theory and had actually been made at the time of the murders. Graysmith's new spin, however, is that he claims that Gibson was also Jack the Ripper, working with a partner, and theorises that he may have murdered Carrie Brown as well.

Sometime in late 1888, according to Gibson himself, he left Scotland and travelled to North America, arriving in December of that year. Graysmith makes the claim that Gibson landed in New York and then journeyed to New Brunswick, New Jersey, where he served as pastor of a church and was thus in the vicinity of New York City on the night of the 23/24 April, 1891.

Once again, here is a man who has been put forth as a Ripper suspect and who was also in the U.S. at the time of the Brown murder. Is there any other less tenuous connection? Interestingly, aspects of Gibson's description fit closely with that of "C. Kniclo." The pastor was described as being 32 years old in 1891, five-foot nine-inches tall and fair-haired with a small, sandy moustache. Gibson, however, also *"had a wide round face, but was a full-blooded, broad-shouldered, athletic fellow, who, though stubby, was well built."*[39] This is not the slim build of the killer. Nor does Gibson have the long pointed nose or German accent that Miniter described. Gibson had a soft Scottish accent instead and *"effeminate in both voice and manner, Gibson spoke like a gentleman or lord..."*[40]

Of real importance, however, is the question whether Gibson was even in New York on the night of the 23/24 of April. Records only stated that Gibson ministered for some unknown length of time in New Brunswick. Although Graysmith makes the claim that this was New Brunswick, New Jersey, and not the Canadian Province nor one of the two towns in Indiana with this name, there is no evidence that proves this to be true or shows that Gibson was there in 1891.

According to Gibson, sometime soon after he arrived in New York he made his way to California, ministering first in Red Bluff for three and a half years before moving to Chico. He was then offered, and accepted, the post as minister of Emmanuel Baptist Church in San Francisco, delivering his first sermon there on 11 November, 1894. As there is no real reason to doubt Gibson's veracity regarding this information, and no evidence which disproves it, he probably was in Red Bluff California on the night of 23/24 April, 1891, when Carrie Brown was murdered. The existing records do not contradict this.

In the final analysis, there is absolutely no credible evidence linking the Reverend John George Gibson to the Whitechapel Murders and no reason to suspect him of the murder of Carrie Brown.

THE DANISH FARMHAND

When Governor Benjamin B. Odell pardoned Ameer Ben Ali on the 16th of April, 1902, almost eleven years to the day of Carrie Brown's murder, he did so partially because of evidence that pointed the finger at another man.

A year earlier a farmer who lived in Cranford, New Jersey, came forward and claimed that at the time of the Brown murder he had in his employ a Danish farmhand. On the night of the murder, this farmhand was absent from Cranford but returned the next day, the 24th of April, 1891, disappearing for good that very night. The farmer swore that the Dane had left behind a *"peculiar"* key. The farmer had read about the murder and knew that the key to room 31 had disappeared with the killer. This, coupled with the immediate disappearance of the farmhand, led the farmer to suspect some involvement in the murder. For some unstated reason the farmer decided to say nothing about his suspicions until a newspaper reporter contacted him about the matter in 1901.

What are we to make of this story? It seems likely that a blond Danish farmhand might be confused with a blond German but, unfortunately, we have no other description of this man to go by. Interestingly, if the farmer's story was false and he was just motivated to attempt to help Ben Ali by making the whole thing up, then why invent a Danish farmhand? Why not claim that the man was in fact German? This may indicate that the farmer was telling the truth as he knew it. Unfortunately there is not much to go on here. Although the fact that the Dane was absent from Cranford on the night of the murder and then disappeared immediately afterwards is interesting, it is not conclusive.

The real question is whether or not the farmer was telling the truth. Why did he wait for ten years to pass before coming forward? How was it that a reporter got wind of the farmer's suspicions? As the story really offers nothing in the way of solid proof for anything, why did Governor Odell see it as mitigating evidence against Ben Ali's guilt?

The answer probably lies in the fact that Ben Ali's conviction had never sat well with a large percentage of the population. Several important individuals were seeking Ben Ali's release, including the French Ambassador, and this, coupled with a discriminating look at the evidence (especially the blood evidence), offered Odell an excuse to pardon the Algerian. Looked upon this way, the tale of the Danish farmhand may or may not be true, but, regardless, it fulfilled its purpose and helped lead to the full pardon of Ameer Ben Ali.

ARBIE LA BRUCKMAN
a.k.a.: John Francis, John Frank, John Frenchy, Frenchy, Frenchy No. 2

Arbie La Bruckman was a contemporary suspect in the murder of Carrie Brown and was, for a brief time, Chief Inspector Byrnes' prime suspect. Indeed, he was the man referred to at Chief Inspector Byrnes' 25th of April press conference, of which the press later said: *"...he believes that when he gets this man he will have the murderer."*[41]

Known only as "Frenchy No. 2" during most of the investigation, La Bruckman's real name was reported only briefly and then, slipping through the cracks of history, was long forgotten. Rediscovered by Michael Conlon, who has written three articles on the subject,[42] La Bruckman's name has been linked, by Mr. Conlon, with not only the murder of "Shakespeare" but also the Whitechapel murders as well.

Not much is now known about the personal history of this suspect. La Bruckman himself stated to the press that he was born in Morocco in 1862 and was thus around 26 years old in 1888, the time of the Whitechapel murders, and roughly 29 at the time of the Brown murder. He and his family arrived in New York in 1870 when he was eight years old, and the majority of his life was spent living as an American.

According to the *Daily Continent,* by the age of 15 La Bruckman was making his living as a cattleman working for the National Steam Navigation Company, known more widely as the National Line,

crossing the Atlantic between New York and the British ports of London and Liverpool.

An unknown informant, who was quoted in the *New York World* on the 30th of April, 1891, stated that, *"...the sailors on the cattle ships tell horrible stories of his cruelty to the dumb brutes in his care. When one of these animals would break a leg or receive some injury that necessitated its slaughter, 'Frenchy,' they say, would take apparent delight in carving it up alive while the sailors looked on. No one dared oppose him, his temper was so bad."*[43] Interestingly, this informant had also stated, incorrectly, that La Bruckman had been crossing the Atlantic for only the last two or three years. This may be an indication that this anonymous source did not know La Bruckman as well as we have been led to believe.

By 1891 Arbie La Bruckman was a foreman of drovers and slaughterman and the sole supporter of his mother and sister who lived on Water Street, the same street as the East River Hotel. Arbie La Bruckman himself had no fixed address but lived, when not at sea, at several different lodging houses in and around New York City.

As to his movements around the time of the murder, La Bruckman arrived back in New York from an Atlantic crossing on a National Line steamer, the 4,512 ton *S. S. Spain,* on the 10th of April. At this time he went to live at 81 James Street, which was situated just two blocks from the East River Hotel. It was claimed by one source quoted in the press that, in the days just before the murder of Carrie Brown, La Bruckman had been working in John Speekmann's saloon at the corner of Oliver and Oak Streets, the same saloon that Ameer Ben Ali, Frenchy No. 2, Mary Ann Lopez and Carrie Brown were said to have been seen drinking in on the night of the 23rd. It is uncertain whether this information was correct, but Speekmann's saloon was situated only a short block from where La Bruckman had been staying on James Street. What is known is that at some point around the time of the murder he moved to New Jersey after he found work in the Central Stock Yards in Jersey City.

La Bruckman was arrested at the stock yards by New Jersey Police Detective Close at noon on Wednesday the 29th of April 1891. New York was notified of the arrest, but it took several hours before anyone was sent to interview the prisoner. At 3:00 pm detective Sergeant George McClusky finally arrived. After a talk with the New Jersey police, he questioned La Bruckman briefly and then told the incredulous Jersey cops to release the man. They were reluctant to do so but were finally convinced, and La Bruckman was released.

On Saturday the 9th of May, La Bruckman took ship on the *S. S. Buffalo* and seemingly disappeared from history.

As a suspect in the Brown murder, La Bruckman's name can stand on its own but Mr. Conlon has buttressed his theory that La Bruckman was the murderer of "Shakespeare" by connecting him with the Whitechapel murders. La Bruckman thus becomes yet another suspect whose guilt partially hinges on the possibility that he was also Jack the Ripper. The merits of this assertion are tenuous at best.

There are a couple of sources that link Arbie La Bruckman's name with the Whitechapel crimes. The most interesting and detailed is the anonymous source quoted in the *New York World* referred to earlier. This source claimed that *"There is a man named 'Frenchy' who answers the description of Frenchy No. 2, and who was arrested in London about a year and a half ago in connection with the Whitechapel murders... When he was arrested on suspicion that he was 'Jack the Ripper' he knocked down the officer who tackled him and made things*

very lively for half a dozen men before they got him under arrest."

The problem with this and other sources is not so much the anonymity of the informant, although that is worrisome, but with the simple fact that we have no idea how the informant came by this information. If the information had come from some first hand knowledge of La Bruckman's arrest then it is important and must be given due deference. If, however, the infor-

Arbie La Bruckman a.k.a. "Frenchy No. 2"

Image from *The New York World*

mation came from La Bruckman himself then this is not an indication that the story is true, only an indication that La Bruckman told this story. It is one thing to **claim** that this source is actually corroborating La Bruckman's tale independently but another thing to prove it.

We do, of course, know that La Bruckman did indeed freely offer his own version, or versions, of the events surrounding his supposed arrest in London to both the police and the press. When his story is examined closely, however, serious flaws are revealed.

The earliest press version of La Bruckman's tale of being arrested as Jack the Ripper that I could find appeared in the *Brooklyn Eagle* when a reporter was able to interview the New Jersey police on Wednesday the 29th of April, shortly after La Bruckman's arrest and interrogation.

The reporter was able to learn that: *"A man who admits that he is Frenchy No. 2, and one who was held in London for two weeks as 'Jack the Ripper,' when he was discharged for want of evidence, was arrested at noon to-day in Jersey City."* Later in this article the reporter added, *"It was when he went to England on a cattle ship that he was arrested then as 'Jack the Ripper.' He was closely questioned by Scotland yards* (sic) *detectives at that time, but they did not find sufficient evidence to place the responsibility of the Whitechapel crimes on him and therefor they let him go."*

No real details surrounding the arrest are given here, only some facts surrounding his incarceration: he was held for two weeks and then released for want of evidence. This information changes only hours later.

After his release from the New Jersey City lockup, on the same day as his arrest, reporters from other newspapers were able to track La Bruckman down to get his story.

The *New York World* reported that La Bruckman stated: *"...About 11 o'clock one night a little after Christmas, 1889, I was walking along the street I carried a small satchel. I was bound for Hull, England, where I was to take another ship. Before I reached the depot, I was arrested and taken to the London Headquarters. I was locked up for a month, placed on trial and duly acquitted. After my discharge the Govern-ment gave me £100 and a suit of clothes for the inconvenience I had suffered."* [44]

This statement is fleshed out somewhat in a *Daily Continent* article, where it was reported that La Bruckman had *"...freely acknowledged that he was arrested in London eighteen months ago on suspicion of being the Whitechapel murderer. He claims that his trial for killing one of Jack The Ripper's victims lasted two weeks, and when he was acquitted the Government gave him £500 and a new suit of clothes..."* [45]

We now have to ask the question: What really was the length of La Bruckman's incarceration? Was it the two weeks that he initially told the New Jersey police or was it the four weeks followed by a two week trial he told the reporters who tracked him down? If he was telling the truth about the incident then why did he change his story?

Another discrepancy jumps out at even the casual reader of La Bruckman's narrative: the claim that he had been put on trial and charged with being the Whitechapel murderer. The detail of the trial was missing from the *Eagle's* report and indeed changes entirely the circumstances surrounding La Bruckman's release from Scotland Yard's custody. Rather than simply being released because of want of evidence, as he had first claimed, the addition of the trial means that he was released because he was found not guilty and acquitted. There are very few areas of the study of the Whitechapel murders that one can claim an absolute but this is one of them: It is absolutely impossible that this ever happened.

The Whitechapel murders became a world wide sensation with interest spanning international borders, language and culture.

> There are very few areas of the study of the Whitechapel murders that one can claim an absolute but this is one of them: It is absolutely impossible that this ever happened.

The study of these murders has been an almost continuous one, from the death of the very first victim to this date. There is no way, therefore, that a trial, which would have garnered incredible national and international interest, can have gone unreported in its day or, if reported, missed by the students of these crimes. Keeping this in mind, we are therefore left with the simple conclusion that La Bruckman must have been lying when he claimed that he was put on trial for being Jack the Ripper.

In an effort to defuse this glaring flaw in La Bruckman's story, however, Michael Conlon has speculated that perhaps La Bruckman confused some part of his incarceration in a small holding cell with a trial involving judge, jury, lawyers, witnesses and spectators! Surely this confusion would have to stem from a mental deficiency that is otherwise not evident from the known facts.

Mr. Conlon also goes on to point out that this detail of the trial was changed — yet again — in later press reports. *"Two later reports,"* writes Mr. Conlon, *"stated that La Bruckman admitted to being arrested a year and a half earlier... 'in London on suspicion of having killed nine women in the Whitechapel district, but after being in jail for a month was discharged.'"*[46]

Conveniently, in these later reports the untenable detail of the trial has disappeared, but, insteading of instilling any confidence in the truth of Arbie La Bruckman's story, this rather meaningful alteration offers only a feeling of increased misgiving and scepticism.

How long was he held by the London police? Was it two weeks, four weeks or six weeks? If indeed he spent at least six weeks in confinement, one month in police custody, followed by two weeks at trial, what are we to make of not only the trial disappearing from records but with it two weeks of his detention? More questions are raised than answered with these later reports, and we are left with at least three different versions of the circumstances surrounding the cattleman's detention and release.

Suspicions of his untrustworthiness are raised by other elements of La Bruckman's story, including the £100 or £500, another glaring change in the tale, in compensation supposedly offered by the British Government. £100 alone was a small fortune in 1890, and, although I do not doubt that compensation could have been offered, this sum seems incommensurate with the inconvenience suffered. £500 is pure fiction. This view can be illustrated with an example from the casebook of the Whitechapel murders.

In mid June of 1894 Ripper suspect Michael Ostrog was arrested and charged with obtaining three gold watches with chains by false pretenses from a jeweller in Eaton in 1889.[47] He denied the charge, claiming that he had been in prison in France at the time. In July he was committed for trial at which several eye witnesses identified Ostrog as the thief. Found guilty, yet still maintaining his innocence, he was sentenced to prison for five years and incarcerated. Shortly thereafter information arrived from France confirming Ostrog's alibi and proving that at the time of the robbery he had been in custody in the asylum wing of a French prison. Ostrog was released and, after having served some two to three weeks in police custody followed by a trial and then three months in prison, he was awarded the sum of only £10 in monetary compensation.

It is difficult to see how La Bruckman would be awarded ten to fifty times this amount for being held for only two, four, or six weeks, depending on which story you believe, in police custody and without having served any actual prison time.

Mr. Conlon has wondered whether La Bruckman's *"lengthy detention and his American citizenship"*[48] might account for the compensation, but although this thought might reflect today's geopolitical realities this was not the case in early 1890. In 1890 Great Britain was a super power while the United States was not. Going back to the casebook again, one has to look no further than the failed diplomatic attempts from the American Government to free Florence Maybrick as proof.

Starting in 1891 attempts by the highest echelon of the U.S. government were continually rebuffed by Britain. As author Trevor L. Christie has written, *"Probably never in the history of penology have so many persons high and low united in common cause to win freedom for a single prisoner as in the case of Florence Maybrick..."*,[49] and yet that freedom was not won until fifteen years had passed. While Mrs. Maybrick had come from a good American family with some wealth and prestige, in contrast, Arbie La Bruckman was an itinerant sailor and an immigrant from a poor slum family. If Britain was unmoved by the petitions of three American Presidents (Harrison, Cleveland, and McKinley), then why would it be moved to offer La Bruckman such a munificent sum merely because he was an American citizen? The answer is that it wouldn't. This is not to say that La Bruckman could not have received compensation, only that the sum claimed by him is too great to be taken seriously.

This leads to another point regarding this type of restitution. Under what circumstances was monetary recompense offered?

Michael Ostrog

Florence Maybrick

The answer to this question is illuminating. British justice offered monetary compensation in those cases where the innocence of the offender was proved beyond a shadow of a doubt or when mitigating evidence proved a miscarriage of justice. In the case of Michael Ostrog, for instance, he was granted the £10 because the French government provided an iron clad alibi after he had been sent to prison.

Thus if Arbie La Bruckman was telling the truth and he was offered monetary compensation by the British Government as he claimed, then there must have been some overwhelming evidence that proved his innocence. In short, Arbie La Bruckman was not Jack the Ripper and there was irrefutable evidence to prove this. On the other hand, claims of monies granted to him might simply be yet another lie.

Moreover, it should be noted that as of this date no official corroboration has been found for any of La Bruckman's story. No files, police or judicial, no newspaper reports in either the United States or Great Britain, no mention in police reminiscences and absolutely no hint among the Whitechapel murder's case files. This seems odd when we consider that La Bruckman claims that he was held for several weeks as a suspect. This would tend to mean some great police interest in him, evidence of which surely would have appeared somewhere. Unfortunately we are left with a story that, at best, is filled with serious question marks and, at worst, is filled with lies.

As for Conlon's discovery that National Line steamships were docked in London on each of the nights that women were murdered by the Whitechapel killer, although an interesting fact, this hardly constitutes proof of La Bruckman's guilt. It must be kept in mind that the National Line had a dozen ships sailing between the Port of New York and the British ports of London and Liverpool. It is not surprising, therefore, that National Line steamships were docked in London on the dates of the murders, just as they would also be docked in Liverpool and New York and would be in transit on the Atlantic on those same dates. Unless it can be proven that La Bruckman himself was in London on each of the dates of Ripper attacks this fact only offers a tantalising area for further research.

With Arbie La Bruckman's story of being arrested for suspicion of being Jack the Ripper in serious doubt, what then of his place as the possible murderer of Carrie Brown? Serious problems occur here as well.

Two points are important to keep in mind. First, that La Bruckman was in the company of Carrie Brown only hours before her murder (this fact alone would make La Bruckman of extreme interests to the police), and, second, that Mary Miniter was the only person to definitely see Brown with her killer — a man whose name was written into the hotel register as "C. Kniclo."

Here we reach our first huge stumbling block when considering Arbie La Bruckman as Carrie Brown's killer: Arbie La Bruckman does not match the description of "C. Kniclo."

According to Miniter the man who rented the room with "Shakespeare" was *"about thirty-two to thirty-five years of age. He was about 5 feet 8 ½ inches tall and slim in build. He had a long sharp nose and a heavy blond mustache. He wore a dark-brown cutaway coat, dark trousers and a battered derby hat.... I thought the man was a German."*[50]

Newspaper descriptions of La Bruckman, however, state that, *"He is a villainous-looking man of about twenty-nine years and of remarkably strong physique. He is about 5 feet 7 inches in height and weighs about 180 pounds, has black hair and a dark brown mustache...,"* and that he was a *"miniature Hercules"* with *"big cheek bones, a prominent nose and very large mouth. His neck is like a bull's and there is not an ounce of spare flesh on his wiry frame. The tendons stand out on his arms like gas pipes."*[51] La Bruckman was reported as wearing a sailor's cloth cap, blue coat, calico shirt and coarse, dark trousers.

Certain discrepancies between the descriptions fall within acceptable limits of variance. That La Bruckman was about 29 years old while "C. Kniclo" was estimated as being 32 to 35, for example, is interesting but not conclusive. The height difference, on its own, is also not convincing enough to convict or exonerate La Bruckman, but perhaps the two points together might offer the beginning of some doubt. This doubt is intensified, however, when we compare the other information offered in the descriptions.

"C. Kniclo" was described by Mary Miniter as having *"a long sharp nose."* La Bruckman's nose was described as being *"prominent,"* and the sketch of him that appeared in the *World* newspaper shows a seemingly large perhaps bulbous nose but one that was not long and certainly wasn't sharp.

Miniter stated that "C. Kniclo" had a *"slim build,"* while a police bulletin stated that the wanted man was *"rather thin."* La Bruckman, on the other hand, was described as being a *"miniature Hercules"* with a *"remarkably strong physique"* and that *"his neck is like a bull's and there is not an ounce of spare flesh on his wiry frame. The tendons stand out on his arms like gas pipes."* It is impossible to see how a man of this build could be described as being *"rather thin."*

Michael Conlon points out that part of the description includes the observation that *"...there is not an ounce of spare flesh on his wiry frame,"* which leads him to suggest that *"'Wiry frame' would certainly not suggest brawniness, but rather, slenderness."*[52] Mr Conlon, however, seems to ignore the more telling information that La Bruckman was described as *"...about 5 feet 7 inches in height and weighs about 180 pounds..."* and of solid muscle if the rest of the description is to be believed. 5 feet 7 inches in height and 180 pounds in weight are not the measurements of a "slim," "slender,"or "rather thin" man.

Any lingering doubts that we are discussing two different men should be dispelled by the difference in hair colour between "C. Kniclo" and Arbie La Bruckman. "C. Kniclo" was described as having a *"heavy blond mustache"* or *"light coloured"* hair. The cattleman's hair was described as being *"black"* or *"dark"* while his mustache was *"dark brown."*

Although Miniter may have seen the man under less than ideal circumstances, as has been pointed out, it is impossible to believe that black hair and a dark brown mustache can, by some trick of the shadows, appear to be blond or light coloured when viewed in a poorly lit hotel office at night.

And what are we to make of Miniter's observation that the murderer, because of his accent, appeared to her to be German? La Bruckman was born in Morocco but might he originally come from German ancestry? Mr Conlon has pointed out that he had some sort of accent but it is unknown what kind. There are, however, some clues that point to France being his ancestral point of origin.

La Bruckman was not a native indigenous Moroccan but came from a European background. Although Morocco in the nine-teenth century was an independent nation, its strategic importance and economic potential sparked an intense and often violent rivalry between France (which already had assumed control of neighboring Algeria), Spain, and Germany. This situation lasted until 1912 when France finally won out and most of Morocco became a French protectorate.

La Bruckman was not known to have spoken German, but it was claimed by people that knew him that he spoke French, as well as English and Arabic. It seems likely that if he spoke French it was because he came from a French background. This would explain not only the nickname, "Frenchy," which was applied to him, but also his close friendship with Amcer Ben Ali. Ben Ali had not only come from Algeria, Morocco's neighbour, but had fought for France in the Franco Prussian War and also spoke some French.

It is also interesting to note that in 1891 the press stated that people who knew him believed that La Bruckman's accent was Alsatian. Presumably this was not wild speculation. They didn't throw a dart at a map of Europe, or, baring the off chance that Professor Henry Higgins was actually working in the slums of New York in 1891, make a dialectological assumption based upon his unknown accent. A connection to Alsace seems to be information that was likely to have come from La Bruckman himself.

The region of Alsace, originally part of Charlemagne's Carolingian Empire, came under Swabian (German) control by 870. In 1648, after the Thirty Years War and with the Treaty of Westphalia, Alsace came under almost complete French control, with total control achieved by 1697. This Franco/Germanic history seems to be reflected in La Bruckman's name where the French prefix "La" is added to the German sounding name "Bruckman."

French control over the provinces of Alsace and Lorraine was maintained until after the Franco-Prussian war of 1870, at which point the defeated French were forced to cede the territory back to Germany. (It may be relevant that the year 1870 not only saw an exodus of Alsatians from Alsace, many of whom fled to the United States, but that this was also the year that La Bruckman's family arrived in the U.S.). French control was re-exerted after the Treaty of Versailles. If, therefore, Arbie La Bruckman's family was indeed Alsatian then he can be considered to be French in origin and not German and would not have a noticeable German accent.

Based on the description offered by Mary Miniter we have to conclude that "C. Kniclo" and Arbie La Bruckman were two separate individuals.

Or do we? What of talk that Miniter offered more than one description of the killer? Arguing that Miniter's description is untrustworthy, Michael Conlon states that *"Miniter ... gave at least two somewhat dissimilar descriptions of the man who accompanied Brown on the fateful night"* and also states that this is *"a fact."*[53] This is apparently based on reports found in the *New York Herald,* 25, 26 April, 1891 and the *Daily Continent,* 25 April, 1891 which did indeed offer a **slightly** different description of "C. Kniclo." The *"somewhat dissimilar"* descriptions consist of changing the hair colour from "blond," or "light," to "light brown" and "brown."

It would be difficult to argue, however, that this is an example of Miniter's untrustworthiness or that she deliberately changed

Mary Miniter

From *The New York World*

her story and so clouded the issue of identification of the suspect that she can't be trusted.

It must be remembered that the majority of the newspapers offered their readers very similar descriptions of the killer: a blond, thin, long nosed German. It should also be recalled that the police unfailingly followed this description of the suspect. From police bulletins to the type of men arrested and brought in for questioning, there was a consistency on the part of the police of investigating men who were blond. Inspector Byrnes himself later told reporters that *"[C. Kniclo] ... was described by Mary Miniter as being blond."*[54]

This search for a blond suspect was so dogmatic that anytime the police deviated from it reporters commented on it. Evidence of this can be seen in the arrest of Eli Commanis who was described as being *"dark and short"* in one report, or having *"dark brown hair"* in another, and who reporters pointed out *"does not answer the description sent out by the New York police..."*[55] Even the *World* reporter who interviewed Arbie La Bruckman commented, *"He is very far, however, from answering the description of the murderer given out by the New York police."*[56]

The evidence clearly points to a doggedness on the part of the police that belies any question of more than one description of the killer having been made by Mary Miniter. Questions were raised about descriptions made by other witnesses but overall the police investigation stuck with Miniter's blond German. As one reporter stated after the investigation was over, *"...there have been dozens of light complexioned men with long noses and blond moustaches placed under arrest in this and other cities."*[57]

The strong possibility exists that the slightly different descriptions offered in the Herald and the Daily Continent do not reflect a changing story offered by Mary Miniter but rather might simply be chalked up to reporting error — an opinion that anyone who has studied the London press reports surrounding the Whitechapel murders will easily understand.

Of course this would all be moot if Mary Miniter was lying about "C. Kniclo's" description as has been suggested.

The day before Chief Inspector Byrnes announced that Ameer Ben Ali had been charged with the murder of Carrie Brown doubts, conveniently, began to appear in the press that Miniter may not be as truthful a witness as one would like.

"It was somehow learned that [Miniter] *has not given a correct description of the man who was last seen with the woman who was murdered. It is hinted that she may be actuated by motives to shield the fellow, who was an acquaintance of hers."*[58]

Chief Inspector Byrnes went even further and, in an exercise in character assassination overkill, stated that Miniter was not only an alcoholic and a prostitute but, according to the *World,* she was also *"an opium fiend, and has associated with Chinamen."*[59] The average New York reader would get the point.

To trust the word of an alcoholic prostitute was bad enough but one who was also a drug fiend who associated with "Chinamen," thus a woman who paid no heed to the dangers faced by the people of the United States from the "yellow peril," was unthinkable. Fear of the "inscrutable Chinese" along with a general distrust of Asian immigration had led to the Chinese Exclu-

sion Act of 1882, which prohibited all Chinese persons, along with "lunatics" and "idiots," from entering the United States for ten years. The ban on Chinese immigration was extended in 1888 and again in 1892. Seen with today's eyes Byrnes' remark would be equivalent to claiming that your prime witness was a crack whore with ties to Muslim extremists – a description not exactly designed as a show of trust and support.

The day after Ameer Ben Ali was charged with the murder of Carrie Brown, Byrnes once more commented on Miniter's trustworthiness and in a revealing interview made the statement, *"She has admitted to me that she deliberately lied in her description and now says it was given on the spur of the moment."*[60] The lead investigator had unequivocally confirmed the suspicions, fed to the newspapers by the police, that Mary Miniter had lied all along about the description of "C. Kniclo."

Or did she? We will look at Byrnes' interview and the disinformation contained in it a little later on in this article and focus on the fact that Chief Inspector Byrnes and his men were under an incredible amount of pressure, to say nothing of world scrutiny, to solve the murder. As the days passed it became clear that the murderer, "C. Kniclo," was not going to be found easily or quickly and possibly never at all. The decision was made that, in order to save face, a scapegoat should be found and charged. Ameer Ben Ali became this scapegoat. He was a foreigner, had a bad reputation and, best of all, was already under lock and key.

There were problems with this course of action, however. Chief among them was that in order for the case to be made against an innocent man, the New York Detective Bureau first had to do something about their eyewitness, Mary Miniter, and her damning description of the inconveniently suspect "C. Kniclo."

Chief Inspector Thomas Byrnes

Woodcut from an 1889 issue of *Harper's Weekly*

How could Ben Ali be guilty if he was not the man who rented the room with Carrie Brown? What happened to the suspect "C. Kniclo" who the police had been actively searching for but had never found? These were annoying questions that Chief Inspector Byrnes had to deflect. His response was that the suspect, "C. Kniclo," didn't matter as new evidence proved Ben Ali's guilt. Besides, Byrnes claimed, the police now had absolutely no hope of finding, let alone identifying, the earlier suspect as the name "C. Kniclo" was made up. The eyewitness, Miniter, had not only lied about his description but she was also one of the lowest dregs of society and her word was absolutely worthless. In fact the man was totally innocent (although never interrogated or cleared or able to give an account of himself), according to Inspector Byrnes, apparently without a shred or proof or scrap of evidence to support this view. The man had simply vanished into the filth and stench of a Fourth Ward night leaving no name or description to mark his passing.

Mr. Conlon has written, *"Should anyone suggest that Miniter's description was being negated so as to 'fit-up' Ali for eventual prosecution, I would simply point out that there is no evidence whatsoever, beyond mere speculation, that this was the case."*[61] Yes, perhaps, but not idle speculation. It is instead a speculation based on the facts of the case and one overwhelming piece of evidence: the statement made by Night Clerk Kelly of the Glenmore Hotel.

If Mary Miniter had indeed deliberately lied to Chief Inspector Byrnes and her description had been "given on the spur of the moment" then how do we explain Kelly's description of the bloodstained man who entered his hotel on the early morning of the murder? Kelly's description matches exactly with that of Miniter's: *"The fellow spoke with a pronounced German accent ... about five feet nine inches in height, light complexion, long nose, and light mustache. He says that he wore a shabby cutaway coat and a shabby old derby hat."*[62]

Are we to believe that Kelly was also just making this up on the spur of the moment? Or are we to believe, as was suggested with Miniter, that he was covering for someone? If that was the case then all he had to do when the police asked him if anything unusual had happened at the Glenmore on the morning of the murder was to say no, nothing had happened, and watch the detectives walk out the door.

What about the Glenmore's night watchman, Tiernan, who also saw the bloodstained man? Was he part of the conspiracy as well? If Kelly and Tiernan were working in concert with Miniter then why were they not punished once Miniter's supposed deceit had been exposed? For that matter, why was Miniter herself never punished for obstruction of justice and misleading a police investigation? Why was she even allowed to give evidence at both the inquest and the trial if she was such a mendacious and untrustworthy witness?

As I have shown, it seems likely that Kelly was interviewed by the police sometime in the early morning hours of Saturday the 25th of April before the newspapers had hit the stands with news of the murder and Mary Miniter's description of the murderer. Kelly's description, if one believes it, thus corroborates Miniter's and shows that the man who rented the room with "Shakespeare" was not Arbie La Bruckman but the long nosed, blond haired German whom Kelly, interestingly, stated spoke *"broken English."* La Bruckman had lived in the United States for most of his life and so it is hard to see that he could have spoken only broken English.

We are not finished with the Glenmore Hotel. It was discovered by reporters that Arbie La Bruckman had at one time lived at the Glenmore. It was suggested that, as he was covered in blood after the murder, La Bruckman would logically return to a place that he knew in order to find a safe haven and a place where he could wash himself. La Bruckman's connection with the hotel disproves this theory rather than supports it.

The New York police headquarters

Why would a murderer, covered in his victim's blood, make his way to a place where he could be recognized and easily identified to the police? Neither night clerk Kelly nor night watchman Tiernan recognized the blood-stained man although one would assume one or the other would have known La Bruckman. More damning, why would a blood-stained La Bruckman, after leaving the scene of the murder on Catherine Slip and Water Street, make his way to the Glenmore when his own mother and sister lived down the street from the East River Hotel on Water? Surely this was a safer bet for refuge and concealment.

In the end, however, the fact remains that Arbie La Bruckman, or actually "Frenchy No. 2," was named by Inspector Byrnes as the murderer of Carrie Brown. This is the main argument surrounding his guilt but, as we have seen in part two of this

article,[63] there was more to this declaration than meets the eye.

Experienced police reporters noted that Byrnes released this conclusion after a mysterious man, handcuffed and led by a police captain and two detectives, was taken first to Police Headquarters and then to Oak Street, the command post for the Brown murder investigation. This arrest seems to have caused a flurry of police activity in which all the witnesses, locked up in the House of Detention, were transported back to Oak Street to be re-interviewed. Byrnes then called his press conference.

The reporters, who well knew the Chief Inspector and his methods, were suspicious of Byrnes' reasons for calling this assembly. They concluded that the Chief of Detectives must already have his suspect in custody, probably the handcuffed man, and that the news conference was nothing more than a publicity stunt, something Byrnes had pulled in the past. They were shocked, however, when, the very next day, Byrnes and his men, rather than displaying the captured suspect, were back on the streets reinvestigating ground already covered and were described as being in an irritable mood.

Something had happened to the investigation between the time of the press conference on Saturday night and the few short hours before the start of the next day. Something that had, apparently, sent the NYPD back to square one and made Chief Inspector Byrnes quickly backpedal away from any question that "Frenchy No. 2" was the murderer. So much so that as early as Monday, Byrnes was denying that he had ever said that "Frenchy No. 2" was anything more than a suspect.

It seems likely, therefore, that there never was any concrete proof against La Bruckman and what evidence there was quickly became problematic.

It is perhaps here that I should discuss a piece of information brought up by Michael Conlon regarding the identification of "C. Kniclo" by Mary Miniter. According to an article published in the *New York Herald* after Mary Miniter was re-interviewed by Byrnes, on the night of the press conference, she positively identified "C. Kniclo" as being "Frenchy No. 2," a fact that Mr. Conlon uses as proof that Arbie La Bruckman was identified as the murderer of Carrie Brown.

The article discusses the witnesses, who describe "Frenchy" and his "cousin," and states, *"When the inspector heard the women's story, he sent again for Mamie Minetur* (sic)*, the woman who let the couple into the hotel that night, and questioned her about it. She then recalled the fact that 'Frenchy' was in the house that night, and that she recognized the man who came in with the murdered woman as 'Frenchy's' cousin."*[64]

If this was true and the only eye witness at the hotel positively identified "C. Kniclo" as "Frenchy No. 2" then the entire mystery of who killed Carrie Brown is solved. The information provided in the *Herald* is absolutely key to Mr. Conlon's theory that Arbie La Bruckman was the murderer. However there are several things about this article that do not ring true.

Firstly, if you believe Mary Miniter was an untrustworthy witness, that she was *"wholly unreliable"* and with a *"highly questionable veracity"* as Michael Conlon has claimed,[65] then she offers little comfort to those, like Mr. Conlon, who also want to believe that she truthfully identified Arbie La Bruckman as the murderer. Either she was an untrustworthy witness who constantly lied to the police or she was telling the truth and her description of "C. Kniclo" rules out Arbie La Bruckman. Mr. Conlon has even gone so far as to refute that Miniter even clearly saw the man with "Shakespeare," stating in a recent posting on the *Casebook* website that *"under oath, on the stand at the Coroner's Trial, Mary Miniter admitted that the description was **invented, misleading** and **she did not know how the man really looked**"* (emphasis Conlon's). If Mr. Conlon believes this to be true, then how can he state that Miniter positively identified La Bruckman as "C. Kniclo"?

Secondly, and more importantly, this positive identification by Miniter was not published in other newspaper reports of Inspector Byrnes' statement to the press. Indeed one paper took the **opposite** view only days later stating, *"It is generally believed now that the police were at sea in placing suspicion on Frenchy No. 2 .... Mary Minitor* (sic) *... never saw the man who accompanied old 'Shakespeare' on the night she was murdered until he appeared at the hotel with her that night. Frenchy No. 2 was a regular visitor at the hotel and she knew him well."*[66]

As the statement published in the *Herald* was presented in what we would today call a press conference, it is hard to see how the other 30 or so reporters present could miss a piece of information of such importance. We do know, however, that some reporters were offered bits and pieces of information on the night of the 25th. This occurred as witnesses were being taken in and out of Captain O'Connor's private office and before the official statement was made. It is not impossible, therefore, that the Herald was able to "scoop" the other newspapers, but it does not explain why this crucial bit of information was apparently not mentioned at the press conference itself. It is also unclear why Chief Inspector Byrnes would, within hours, start to distance himself from the announcement that "Frenchy No. 2" was the murderer if his main eyewitness had made a positive identification.

It appears that the Herald reporter might have been putting two and two together and coming up with five. As in: Mary Miniter saw the murderer; Miniter was reinterviewed by the police on Saturday night; the police announce on Saturday night that the murderer is "Frenchy No. 2," therefore Miniter must have identified the murderer as being "Frenchy No. 2."

However, there does remain the possibility that Mary Miniter had indeed stated that the man who entered the East River Hotel with "Shakespeare" on the night of the murder was in fact Arbie La Bruckman, but that this information was proved to be false. As it was.

If Mary Miniter had indeed identified Arbie La Bruckman as the murderer, then she was lying. It was proved to the satisfaction of Chief Inspector Byrnes and the New York Police that Arbie La Bruckman had an alibi for the night of the murder. When Carrie Brown was entering the East River Hotel with "C. Kniclo" La Bruckman was in his Jersey City lodging house.

Chief Inspector Byrnes talks of *"the people that he was living with"* (plural) in Jersey City who corroborated this alibi and stated that, *"Frenchy No. 2, who was supposed to be the man, gave information that, on investigation, showed that he was four miles away from the hotel at the time the murder was committed. Then he was let go."*[67]

This alibi fits nicely with the events of the night. We know that the two couples, Ben Ali with Mary Ann Lopez and La Bruckman with Carrie Brown, were seen drinking together. Brown was next seen entering the East River Hotel with Mary Healey sometime between 9 and 10 o'clock, and Ben Ali entered the hotel, alone, at 11 o'clock. Why had the party ended so early, and why was Brown not with La Bruckman? She had no money and desperately needed a client. His absence might be explained by La Bruckman having to leave New York early in order to get back to Jersey City. The next day was a Friday and presumably he had to go to work at his job at the Central Stock Yards.

Therefore, as the evidence shows, Arbie La Bruckman was innocent of the murder of Carrie Brown.

One last word on La Bruckman. Those who are unconvinced by my arguments exonerating Arbie La Bruckman and who

The East River Hotel

From *The New York World*

believe that the police did have eyewitness proof to support him as the murderer would have to resolve the problem of why the police would feel that it was much easier to frame Ameer Ben Ali, an innocent man, rather than charge the guilty party. Why manufacture evidence, force witnesses to change their stories, or find witnesses who would back up the police version of events rather than merely relying on evidence that supposedly proved "Frenchy No. 2's" guilt? Not enough evidence to actually prove La Bruckman's guilt, yet the police know that he is guilty? Then why not fabricate evidence against La Bruckman just as they did against Ben Ali? It might be illegal, not that Chief Inspector Byrnes seemed to care, but at least the guilty man would be apprehended and punished.

Also, at the time of the La Bruckman arrest the fabrication of a case against Ben

"C. Kniclo"

An artist's rendition from
*Jack the Ripper in New York;
or, Piping a Terrible Mystery*
by W.B. Lawson, 1891

Ali had just begun, possibly on the very same day, and was nowhere near complete. Indeed the police were forced to ask the Coroner to push back the start of the inquest by two weeks in order to firm up their evidence. As this was the case it seems improbable that they would allow a supposedly vicious killer to walk free merely because they had very recently started the wheels in motion against some other, innocent, person.

"C. KNICLO"

What of "C. Kniclo," the man who entered the East River Hotel with Carrie Brown on the night of the murder? It seems clear that he was Brown's murderer, whoever he was, but what do we know about him? Precious little, I'm afraid. We have a description, refuted by some, and an uncertain name, also refuted.

If we trust the description offered by Mary Miniter before she was detained and muzzled by the police, we have a thin, blond haired man with a thick light coloured mustache. He was in his early thirties, stood about 5 feet 8 to 5 feet 9 inches tall with a long and pointed nose, and his accent betrayed him as being German. It is perhaps important that Kelly, the night clerk of the Glenmore Hotel, also thought that the man he saw was German, so this point might be taken as credible. Kelly, who corroborates Miniter's description to the letter, added that the man spoke broken English, indicating someone who had not lived for a long period of time in America.

Added to this we have a description of his clothing: a dark-brown cutaway coat, black trousers, and an old, battered black derby hat. If he was a sailor, and the area around the East River Hotel was a sailor's haunt huddled close to the docks on the East River, he was not typically dressed like one.

What does the name "C. Kniclo" tell us? Again, very little. There is no evidence to support the belief that this was the murderer's real name, which is why I have always used quotation marks around it, and there is some evidence that the name was faked.

Although by law all hotels in New York had to keep a registration book listing the names of their guests, this was not always strictly observed especially in a Fourth Ward dive like the East River Hotel, which catered to prostitutes and their clients. The East River Hotel had already been closed down by the police on more than one occasion because it had ignored this ordinance, as had the Glenmore. Mary Miniter actually gave evidence at Ben Ali's trial that the names had not been recorded on the night of the 23rd of April:

"'...I did not put the names in the hotel register that night, and next morning Tommy Thompson told me to say that C. Kniclo and wife occupied room No. 31 the night before. I did not put it down in the register.' Miniter admitted that the name was invented and put in the register by the bartender the following day to 'make it appear right': 'As a matter of fact,' said lawyer House, 'does anyone ever register at the house?' 'No sir,' was the reply. 'Then you lied to the police when you told them the man registered as Kniclo?' 'I did,' was the frank admission. 'I did so because I was ordered to do so by the bartender and Mr. Jennings, the proprietor.'"[68]

So this testimony makes the name "C. Kniclo" meaningless other than as a way of characterizing the man who rented the room with Carrie Brown. Or so the police would have us believe.

It is highly suspicious that at the time when Chief Inspector Byrnes desperately needed the populace to forget about the man who had entered the hotel with Brown, he began attacking the character and veracity

of the witness who couldn't fail to remind the public of this inconvenient person. He then stated that this witness had admitted that her description was a lie and, finally, after several weeks in police custody and control, the witness herself claimed that even the man's name was false. In order to frame an innocent man, "C. Kniclo" had to become the man who was not there.

The question not asked is why use the name "C. Kniclo," an apparent misspelling of the name Nicolo or Nicolai? If the day bartender Tom Thompson actually had to come up with a name, why did he pick one that he couldn't even spell properly? Why not use Smith or Jones or some other common name? Also, if no one ever registered at the hotel, then all the names in the registry listed for the night of the 23rd must have been faked on the morning of the 24th of April. If this is true then they make interesting reading.

Guests who rented rooms on the fifth floor that night were listed as James Wilson, D. Connor, J. Buckley and C. Kniclo. Kniclo appears as the only non-British name, and, because of that and the misspelling, it sticks out like a sore thumb.

It is also not clear exactly who supposedly wrote this name in the register. According to trial reports in the newspapers it was Tom Thompson, but an earlier report stated that it was Miniter who had written in the name under Thompson's direction. To cloud things even further, the owner of the hotel, James Jennings, had explained that the night door clerk, Eddie Fitzgerald, had written all the names in the register and even pointed out the fact that all the handwriting was Fitzgerald's.

There is clear evidence that the East River Hotel did not always follow the letter of the law regarding the registration book and the names of its clients, so the name in the register is shrouded in doubt. There is also evidence, however, that the hotel personnel couldn't seem to keep their stories straight regarding this name. Additionally, talk of a fake name directly benefited not only the police and the District Attorney's Office but also Ben Ali's struggling defence team.

It was the defence that drew out Miniter's admission that the name was faked in an attempt to prove that none of the hotel staff were trustworthy and that the names, and more importantly the rooms that they were assigned, were unreliable. If the information in the registration book could be shown to be false then the evidence that Ben Ali had stayed in the room across the hall from the murder room could be refuted. Thus no extra importance should be gleaned from the fact that it was the defence who brought out the claim that the name had been faked.

Having said all that, it is highly unlikely that the name "C. Kniclo" would lead to any revelations about the murderer of Carrie Brown, let alone identify him.

So what happened to "C. Kniclo" after the murder? Who can say? It is apparent that in all probability he left room number 31 after locking the door behind him and slipping the key into his pocket. Rather than go back down the stairs, he seems to have climbed through the scuttle and onto the roof as there was fresh blood on the trap door. From the roof he could have dropped or climbed down to the building next door to the hotel on Water Street and then exited from that building. Alternately, he could have simply used the fire escape that ran down the front of the building, although no blood was found on this route.

Walking the short distance to the corner

> **"No suspicion attaches to him in any way, but not a trace of him has been found since that night..."**
>
> **– Chief Inspector Thomas Byrnes**

he would have turned right, crossed Water Street and headed straight up Catherine Slip. He would soon find that the road merged into Catherine Street, and, continuing west about seven blocks, he would come to Chatham Square, described as being not more than five minutes away from the scene of the murder. A left on Chatham Square would bring him to the flight of steps that marked the entrance to the Glenmore Hotel. Where he went after he stopped off at the Glenmore remains a mystery. According to Chief Inspector Byrnes, however, none of the above had happened.

After Ameer Ben Ali was charged with the murder of Carrie Brown the Chief Inspector was interviewed by a reporter for the *Brooklyn Eagle*. This article, filled with errors and obfuscation, appeared on Friday the 1st of May, 1891, and offers us Byrnes' spin on the question of the guilt or innocence of "C. Kniclo."

The article starts out with the claim that, *"There are but two important links now missing in the chain of evidence I and my men have secured and which has been submitted to the district attorney..."* The first link was the ownership of the knife used to kill Brown. Byrnes states that, *"this has not yet been connected with the prisoner, and it is one of the points on which the detectives are at work."* This was apparently a lie. We know that two days earlier Headquarter Detectives had taken Ben Ali out to the Queens County jail for some sort of identification. It was from this jail that two prisoners, David Galloway and Edward Smith, made the claim that the Algerian had owned a knife exactly like the one used to murder Carrie Brown when he was in prison with them. The police had, therefore, already falsely linked Ben Ali with the knife.

Byrnes was then asked about the second link. He replied, *"The other is a link that may not so easily be found. This is the man who went to the East river hotel on the night before the murder with old Shakespeare and was registered by Eddie Fitzgerald, the clerk, as C. Knicio* (sic). *He occupied room 33* (sic) *with old Shakespeare and left the house before or about midnight. No suspicion attaches to him in any way, but not a trace of him has been found since that night.... If this man comes foreword and admits that he spent a portion of the night with the old woman in room 33* (sic) *his evidence would be important in determining many doubtful incidents connected with this case. It would go far to fix the time, for instance. Now if this man's reputation is even one remove above that of the regular denizens of the slums he will be slow to come forward and admit his shameful association with the old woman. We are trying to find him."*

Amazingly the Chief Inspector now attached no suspicion to "C. Kniclo" in any way but he doesn't explain why, or how, he had reached this conclusion, other than to say that he had left the hotel before or about midnight. Byrnes would also go on to state that "C. Kniclo" *"left the room shortly after midnight,"* and was thus not the murderer. How he left and who saw him leave was not explained, and this is a problem.

On the day of the murder it was determined that no one other than Mary Miniter had seen "C. Kniclo" and Carrie Brown together. No one other than Miniter had seen the two enter the hotel and no one at all had seen "C. Kniclo" exit the hotel. How, then, could Byrnes know when "C. Kniclo" had left the building, especially since he had never found the man, never interviewed him and couldn't clear him from

the investigation until he had?

In order for the man to leave the East River Hotel without climbing on to the roof or out of a window he would have to descend the stairs and pass the office on the first landing. Either Miniter or Eddy Fitzgerald should have been stationed there and would have seen him pass, but neither of them did. Perhaps, though, Miniter and Fitzgerald were busy elsewhere and there was no one manning the office at the time. "C. Kniclo" would then reach the ground floor and the short hallway that led to the front door of the hotel. This he would find locked and would be unable to open it without the key. As he never tracked down hotel staff to unlock the front door he would therefore have to enter the bar through the connecting door in the hallway. From the bar he could have left through the main door or through the door to the ladies room, the small drinking room also known as "the box." Unfortunately for Inspector Byrnes no one saw him enter or leave the bar, and no one other than Miniter knew what he looked like. Even more troublesome was the fact that the two doors to the bar were locked at midnight so he would again have needed a key in order to get out.

There is no apparent way that Byrnes could know when "C. Kniclo" had left the hotel other than to suggest that he might have left sometime before the bar doors were locked at midnight. This supposition ignores the fact that as no one had seen "C. Kniclo" leave the building and blood had been found on the scuttle it seems likely that "C. Kniclo" had left the building via the roof. But how could anyone see this as anything other than highly guilty behaviour?

Byrnes also does not explain his statement that Mary Miniter had purposely lied about the description of "C. Kniclo." What reason did she have to lie if it had turned out that he was totally blameless in the murder? The suppositions for the reasons as to why she would lie were that either Miniter knew who the man was and was thus shielding him or knew who he was but was afraid to give any evidence against him. The later is disproved by the man's supposed innocence while the former would surely lead to a quick identification and interview. This never happened.

In the end, no matter what he claimed, Byrnes could give no satisfactory answer to the question of why Mary Miniter lied, just as he could not state how or when "Kniclo" had left the building. As he couldn't provide "Kniclo" with an alibi, and, as he had never traced the man, he couldn't be exonerated. Therefore clearly he must still be the most viable suspect in the murder of Carrie Brown.

"C. Kniclo" seemingly disappeared into history, never to be heard of again. Or did he? An article that appeared in a Canadian newspaper, the *Saint John Globe* from St. John, New Brunswick, dated 23 July, 1891, describe some intriguing parallels with the murder of Carrie Brown and provides some interesting food for thought:

"JACK THE RIPPER," IN FRANCE.

Two murders similar in character to those ascribed in London to "JACK THE RIPPER" have been committed in Marseilles within a week. A man giving an Italian name twice took rooms accompanied by a woman, and in each case the woman was afterwards found murdered, having been strangled then mutilated. A letter sent to the police stated that these crimes were the beginning of a series.

CONCLUSIONS

So, was "C. Kniclo" actually Jack the Ripper, and should Carrie Brown be considered to be another Ripper victim? The short answer is no.

From the time of the Brown murder until today there have been several arguments for including the New York murder with the Whitechapel series, or if not to actually include it then to at least mention it as a possible Ripper murder. These arguments no longer hold much weight.

One of these arguments was the view that a known British serial killer, Severin Klosowski, had actually lived in the area of New York City at the time of the murder and that Inspector Abberline had given the opinion that Klosowski was a good candidate for being the Ripper. As this article has shown, it appears that Klosowski was probably still in London at the time of the Brown murder. This connection with Whitechapel has thus been severed.

A second argument was based on the cessation of Ripper murders in London after the 9th of November, 1888. The fact that the Ripper murders ended the way they did, with the murderer disappearing never to be heard from again, naturally led to the question of what happened to him. Newspaper reports that began to appear at the end of January, 1889, seemed to offer an answer to this puzzling question. Jack the Ripper had apparently left Britain and had travelled to the Americas.

Reports stated that three women had been brutally murdered in Jamaica in December 1888. Close on the heels of these murders was news of six women butchered in Nicaragua in early 1889 followed by the Brown murder in 1891. A logical assumption, given the evidence, pointed to the Ripper having relocating himself across the Atlantic, first to the Caribbean, and then, working his way north, to New York, leaving a red trail of bodies to mark his passage. The "Shakespeare" murder, therefore, was not an isolated incident but part of a larger series that could be traced right back to London in 1888. We now know that no such series existed.

Stephen Ryder has shown conclusively that the supposed three Jamaican Ripper murders were, in fact, only one and that that murder was definitely solved.[69] On the 28th of December, 1888, Letitia Crawford, a black woman in her mid twenties, was found lying dead at the side of the road between Old Harbour and Spanish Town. She had been hit in the face with a board, suffering massive head and facial injuries, and then had her throat cut. The young man that she had been sharing a cart with, one Benjamin Ranger, was quickly arrested, tried, convicted and hanged for the murder.

As for the Nicaraguan homicides, newspaper reports quickly confessed that both the Jamaican and Nicaraguan murder stories were actually hoaxes supposedly planted in the press by Scotland Yard. The highly unlikely premise was that the London police were attempting to draw out the Ripper by tricking him into responding in blood to reports that he had left London. Somehow, the theory went, the killer might make a mistake, and this might lead to a capture — as opposed to, say, only the murder of several additional women.

This leaves the Brown murder as an uncomfortably isolated case. We are left wondering why the Ripper would stop the London series after the 9th of November 1888 only to pick up again in New York, almost two and a half years later, murder only one woman and then disappear completely, never to be heard from again.

Another argument to include the Brown

Carrie Brown was found with clothing wrapped around her head and her right arm twisted under her body.

From *The New York World*

murder as a possible Whitechapel crime is that, if not the Ripper, then who? The thinking seems to be that only one man, London's Jack the Ripper, could have possibly murdered in this brutal way. This is a rather naive belief with no evidence to support it.

Only two years after the murder in New York, American criminologist Arthur MacDonald and certain French colleagues had completely separated the death of Carrie Brown from those in London. One reason was that other mutilation murders had been committed both before and after those in Whitechapel just as there had been other serial killers before the Autumn of Terror. Jack the Ripper wasn't even the first serial mutilation murderer, a fact lost on some, but he did quickly became the most infamous. To MacDonald and other criminologists both then and today, the Ripper wasn't an omnipresent bogey man who travelled the world murdering women. He was, instead, one of several similar case studies that have to be recognized and acknowledged in order to gain a greater understanding of this type of mutilation murder.

In 1893 MacDonald argued, after studying various similar mutilation murders and also official sources from the Brown murder investigation, that the murder of "Shakespeare" was not the work of Jack the Ripper, for various reasons, and concluded with: *"...All things considered, the method employed by* [Brown's murderer] *was very crude when compared with that of Jack the Ripper."*[70] Noting the differences between the methods of the two killers is an interesting and modern view, and, although MacDonald would have never heard the term "copy cat" to describe a murderer, he certainly understood the concept as it pertained to the Brown murder.

He states, *"Considering the notoriety of the cases of* [Jack the Ripper] *it would not be extraordinary to find that similar acts will occur due to a plague of imitators; because it is precisely the weak minded and depraved which are unable to resist or are drawn to these practices to satisfy their morbid propensities. One can easily explain the similarity of brutalities* [between the Brown and Ripper murders] *by the capacity for imitation on the predisposed nervous systems."*[71] There are, of course, some certain similarities in victimology and modus operandi between the London series and the New York crime but, as MacDonald points out, these can easily be explained by imitation, as the details of the Ripper murders were certainly well reported around the world. The only concrete evidence that can be used to scientifically compare the murders is the autopsy report.

Looked at objectively, it becomes clear that although the type of crime was similar, a mutilation murder with psychosexual overtones, the autopsy report shows that there are important differences.

The ability and skill shown by the London murderer is nowhere evident in the New York murder. London's Ripper showed some anatomical knowledge and it was felt that, *"Obviously the work was that of an expert — of one, at least, who had such knowledge of anatomical or pathological examinations as to be enabled to secure the pelvic organs with one sweep of a knife."*[72] Whether the Ripper had such knowledge is debatable. What is not is the fact that whatever skill the Ripper did possess was sufficient to impress the medical fraternity.

In New York Coroner Schultze stated to reporters that, *"The disemboweling was*

as thoroughly done as though performed by a surgeon.... The cutting was not by any means bunglingly done and the character of the wounds would seem to indicate that the murderer may have had some knowledge of surgery."[73] However no anatomical knowledge was exhibited in the Brown murder, and Coroner Schultze also added that, *"The murderer then appears to have taken both hands, torn aside the body on each side of the ghastly wound and dragged out the entrails scattering them around the bed."*[74] Such an action does not demonstrate the same ability as those displayed by the London killer. This is supported by Assistant Coroner Jenkins, the man who actually performed the autopsy on Carrie Brown, who, contradicting his superior, stated, *"If it was done by a surgeon he was a butcher. It was horrible hacking,"*[75] The autopsy report and the post mortem photographs also disprove Coroner Schultze's assertions of any surgical ability demonstrated.

Another discrepancy between the two murderers is the degree of mutilation performed. The mutilations in the London murders became progressively vicious over time, ending in a crescendo of violence. Victims had their throats cut and their abdominal cavities opened. They were eviscerated, and organs were removed and taken away. The final victim, Mary Kelly, was found utterly destroyed.

In New York Carrie Brown did not have her throat cut, a highly significant difference between her death and those of her London sisters. This fact alone excluded her as a genuine Ripper victim in the eyes of Scotland Yard, as it is the throat cutting that was seen as the one unifying point in all five of the so called canonical victims.

Although the wounds to Brown were horrible, especially when one is viewing the post mortem photos, only two of them were of a sufficient degree to cause death. They

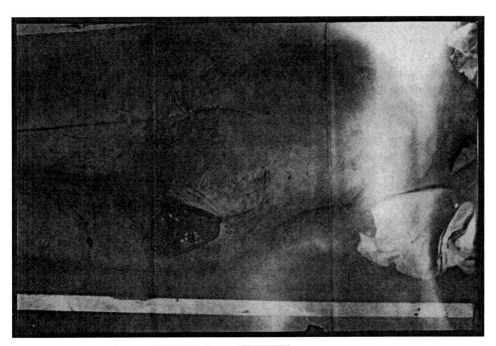

Carrie Brown's morgue photographs

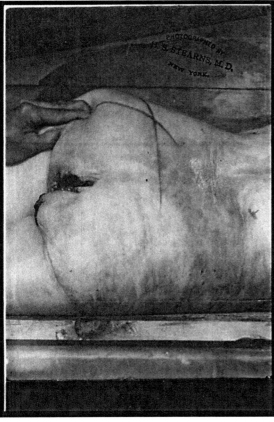

Top: The front view of Carrie Brown's corpse. The photographer apparently reversed the image when making the print, as the wounds show up on the opposite side of the body from where they were indicated in the autopsy report. We have flipped the orientation of the photo so it matches what the doctors described..

Bottom: The main wound went clear through the body. The cuts forming an X-shaped mark on the skin can also be seen.

Photos courtesy New York City Municipal Archives

do not resemble the much more horrific wounds to the bodies of the Whitechapel victims in either degree or scope. Even more damning is the fact that most of the wounds suffered by Brown were extraneous cuts, and some were mere scratches. Her abdominal cavity was not opened, but rather a deep gash was made to her left side. Because of this relatively small wound (at least in relation to the Whitechapel victims), "Shakespeare" was not eviscerated, although two pieces of her intestines were pulled out and scattered on the bed. This is not the same methodology used by London's Jack the Ripper, who opened the body fully and removed the intestines, which were in the way, in order to obtain sexual and internal organs.

In Brown's case her left ovary was found lying on the bed, but, given the nature and position of the *"penetrating wound"* to her left side, it is impossible to say whether this extraction was done purposely or if it was merely an accidental outcome of this wound. Certainly it seems highly unlikely that the man who removed *"the uterus and its appendages with the upper portion of the vagina and the posterior two-thirds of the bladder"* and took them away with him, as in the Chapman murder, would be content to merely sever one small ovary from its connections and allow it to simply roll onto the bed when Brown's body was turned onto its side by her killer. This cannot seriously be compared with the organ removal displayed by the London killer.

As the years extended beyond 1888 it seems that almost every woman murdered with a knife was considered as a possible victim of Jack the Ripper. Murders in Mexico, Japan, France, Austria, Germany, Chile, the United States and Britain were either seen as possible Ripper murders or, as time passed, Ripper-like murders. Were they all committed by imitators and copy cats? There had been Ripper-like mutilation murders before the London series, but after it there was a heightened awareness of this type of murder. After all there was a great mystery to be solved — what ever happened to Jack? In the end none of these crimes could be linked back to the London killer. Even the Ripper-like murder of Alice McKenzie in Whitechapel on 17 July, 1889, only eight months after Mary Kelly's death, was rightfully eliminated from the Ripper series by police surgeon Dr. George Bagster Phillips. If Whitechapel's Alice McKenzie wasn't considered a true Ripper victim, then how can New York's Carrie Brown be? The answer is that she can't.

There is not enough evidence or similarity to state with any conviction that London's Jack the Ripper travelled hundreds of miles across the ocean in order to kill New York's Carrie Brown. Her murder remains unsolved, her murderer unknown.

NOTES:

1. The *New York Times,* Saturday 27 June, 1891.

2. Francis L. Wellman, the Assistant District Attorney who prosecuted Ben Ali, stated that he "was a huge specimen of a man fully six feet-five in height." this, like other statements by Wellman, doesn't seem credible. See Francis L. Wellman, *Luck and Opportunity the Recollections of Francis L. Wellman.* The Macmillan Comp., 1938.

3. Arthur MacDonald, Le Criminel-Type dans Quelques Formes Graves de la Criminalité, second edition, Storck, Lyon France, 1893.

4. One French source claimed that he was 53 at the time of his arrest, although where this information came from is unknown.

5. *The Brooklyn Daily Eagle,* 2 July, 1891.

6. Interestingly both Superintendent Murray and Chief Inspector Byrnes had been regimental members of the New York Zouaves during the American Civil War. Thus they had also worn the Zouave uniform of fez, short jacket and red arabic pantaloons that had been patterned after Ben Ali's Algerian uniform.

7. The Kabylie are the indigenous non Arab Berber tribe that inhabits a mountainous region known as Kabylia, or Kabylie in French, whose capital is the city of Tizi-Ouzo.

8. It was claimed that this begging trick had been learned by Ben Ali in Liverpool and London as, apparently, the New York police were laying the groundwork to link Ben Ali with the Ripper murders.

9. Joseph Levy would go on to serve a long and distinguished career as a criminal lawyer but this was to be his very first criminal case.

10. The *Brooklyn Eagle*, 1 May, 1891.

11. The *New York Times*, 1 May, 1891. The newspapers clearly got this wrong as the Uhlenhuth test to determine if a blood sample is human or not was not developed until 1901.

12. *New York Daily Tribune*, 2 May 1891.

13. The *New York Times*, 14 May, 1891.

14. This statement disregards the work done by the city doctors: Edson and Flint who said that the stains were indeed blood and thus provided the reason that Ben Ali was charged with the murder in the first place.

15. A surprising amount. Put in context this would require him to perform one a day, every day, for just over thirty nine years! Leading one to wonder if there were no other qualified doctors in Philadelphia in the second half of the nineteenth century.

16. The *New York Times*, 2 July, 1891.

17. Ibid.

18. The *Philadelphia Press*, 9 July, 1891.

19. Wellman.

20. The *New York Times*, 4 July, 1891.

21. Ibid.

22. Wellman.

23. Mary Ann Lopez gave evidence that one time Ben Ali became so enraged with her that he had bitten her arm. That he didn't use a knife in his rage or even threaten her with one is telling.

24. The *New York Times*, 5 July, 1891.

25. Neal Sheldon has conclusively shown that Klosowski did not move to this location until 1890. See *Ripperana*, October 1993.

26. The ceremony took place at St. Bonifaces German Roman Catholic Church, Union Street, Whitechapel. See Neal Shelden, *Catherine Eddowes Jack the Ripper Victim,* for a lesson in jaw droppingly impressive research.

27. Definitely no relationship to the Ripper victim. See Neal Sheldon, *Annie Chapman Jack the Ripper Victim,* 2001 or *Catherine Eddowes Jack the Ripper Victim,* 2003. Both self published.

28. John Douglas & Mark Olshaker, *The Cases That Still Haunt Us,* Scribner, 2000.

29. After a search of the existing passenger lists, now held in the Public Records Office at Kew, Sugden was unable to find any mention of the Klosowskis listed in records covering March to July 1891. The authors own search in this area is on going.

30. R. Michael Gordon, *The American Murders of Jack the Ripper.* Praeger Publishers, 2003.

31. As evidenced by the information that when she arrived in London her sister and Chapman were already married. As the marriage took place on 29 October, 1889, she must have arrived in August of 1890. She also stated in 1903 she had been living in Britain for thirteen years which would also seem to indicate the year 1890.

32. Hargrave L. Adam, *The Trial of George Chapman,* William Hodge & Comp. 1930.

33. The *New York Times,* 18 January, 1892.

34. The *Mountain Democrat,* 1 April, 1893.

35. The *Brooklyn Eagle,* 4 May, 1865.

36. McClusky was removed from his position after arresting a well connected group of swindlers

37. See Conlon, Michael. "Ripper Redux," *Ripperologist* No. 48, August, 2003.

38. Regnery Publishing Inc.

39. Robert Graysmith, *The Bell Tower The Case of Jack the Ripper Finally Solved...in San Francisco,* Regnery Publishing Inc., 1999.

40. Ibid.

41. The *New York Times,* 26 April, 1891.

42. See Michael Conlon, "A Tale of Two Frenchy's," *Ripperana* No. 34, October 2000. "The Ripper in America," *Ripperologist,* No. 32, December, 2001. "The Carrie Brown Murder

Case: New Revelations," *Ripperologist* No. 46, May, 2003.

43. The *World,* 30 April, 1891.

44. Ibid.

45. The *Daily Continent,* 30 April, 1891.

46. Conlon, "The Ripper in America."

47. See Philip Sugden, *The Complete History of Jack the Ripper,* Carroll & Graf Publishers revised paperback 2002.

48. Conlon, op. cit.

49. Trevor L. Christie, *Etched in Arsenic,* 1969, George G. Harrap & Co. Ltd. London.

50. The *World,* 25 April, 1891.

51. The *World,* 30 April 1891.

52. Conlon, "The Carrie Brown Murder Case: New Revelations."

53. Ibid.

54. The *Brooklyn Eagle,* op. cit.

55. The *Brooklyn Eagle,* 27 April, 1891.

56. The *World,* op. cit.

57. The *Brooklyn Eagle,* 30 April, 1891.

58. The *New York Herald,* 29 April, 1891.

59. The *World,* op. cit.

60. The *Brooklyn Eagle,* 1 May, 1891.

61. Conlon, op. cit.

62. The *New York Times,* op. cit.

63. See *Ripper Notes,* No.17, January, 2003.

64. The *New York Herald,* 26 April, 1891.

65. See *Ripperologist* No. 46.

66. The *Brooklyn Eagle,* 28 April, 1891.

67. The *Brooklyn Eagle,* 1 May, 1891.

68. The *Morning Herold,* 1 July, 1891.

69. See Stephen Ryder, "The Jamaican Jack the Ripper," *Ripperologist* No. 48, August 2003.

70. MacDonald.

71. Ibid.

72. The *Lancet,* 29 September, 1888.

73. The *World,* 25 April, 1891.

74. Ibid.

75. The *Brooklyn Eagle,* 26 April, 1891.

SOURCES

The author would gratefully like to thank researcher Robert McLaughlin for his aid and generosity in supplying research materials and sources.

BOOKS:

Adam, H.L., *Trial of George Chapman,* Notable British Trials Series, William Hodge & Comp. Ltd., 1930.

Asbury, Herbert, *The Gangs of New York: an Informal History of the Underworld,* Alfred A. Knopf, 1928.

Begg, Paul; Fido, Martin; Skinner, Keith, *The Jack the Ripper A-Z,* third paperback edition, Headline, 1996.

Borchard, Edward M., *Convicting the Innocent,* Garden City Publishers, 1932.

Byrnes, Thomas, *1886 Professional Criminals of America,* Chelsea House Publishers, 1969.

Douglas, John; Olshaker, Mark, *The Cases That Still Haunt Us,* Scribner, 2000.

Evans, Stewart; Gainey, Paul, *The Lodger The Arrest and Escape of Jack the Ripper,* Century, 1995.

Evans, Stewart P.; Skinner, Keith, *The Ultimate Jack the Ripper Sourcebook,* Robinson, 2000.

Gordon, R. Michael, *Alias Jack the Ripper Beyond the Usual Whitechapel Suspects,* McFarland & Comp. Inc., 2001.

Gordon, R. Michael, *The American Murders of Jack the Ripper,* Praeger, 2003.

Graysmith, Robert, *The Bell Tower The case of Jack the Ripper Finally Solved...in San Francisco,* Regnery Publishing Inc., 1999.

Harris, Melvin, *The True Face of Jack the Ripper,* Michael O'Mara Books Ltd., 1994.

Lacassagne, Alexandre, *Vacher l'éventreur et les crimes sadiques,* A. Storck, 1899.

Lardner, James; Reppetto, Thomas, *NYPD a City and its Police,* Henry Holt & Comp., 2000.

Lawson, W.B., *Jack the Ripper in New York; or, Piping a Terrible Mystery.* Log Cabin Library Series, Street and Smith Publishing, 1891, reprint the Ripperological Preservation Society, 1996.

Lewis, Alfred Henry, *Nation-Famous New York Murders,* The Pearson Publishing Co., 1914.

MacDonald, Arthur, *Criminology,* Funk & Wagnalls Co., 1893.

MacDonald, Arthur, *Le Criminel-Type dans Quelques Formes Graves de la Criminalité,* second edition, Storck, Lyon France, 1893.

Nash, Jay Robert, *Compendium of World Crime,* Harrap & Co. Ltd., 1983.

Nash, Jay Robert, *Open Files,* McGraw-Hill Book Comp., 1983.

Odell, Robin, *Jack the Ripper in Fact and Fiction,* Harrap & Co. Ltd., 1965.

O'Donnell, Kevin, *The Jack the Ripper Whitechapel Murders,* Ten Bells, 1997.

Pearson, Edmund, *More Studies in Murder,* Harrison Smith and Robert Haas Inc., second edition 1936.

Riis, Jacob, *The Making of an American* (Macmillan & Co. Ltd. 1901).

Rumbelow, Donald, *Jack the Ripper the Complete Casebook,* Contemporary Books, 1988.

Sante, Luc, *Low Life: Lures and Snares of Old New York* (Farrar, Straus, Giroux. 1991).

Shelden, Neal, *Annie Chapman Jack the Ripper Victim,* self published, 2001.

Shelden, Neal, *Catherine Eddowes Jack the Ripper Victim,* self published, 2003.

Steffens, Lincoln, *The Autobiography of Lincoln Steffens,* Harcourt Brace, 1931.

Sugden, Phillip, *The Complete History of Jack the Ripper,* Carroll & Graf Publishers, 2002.

Walling, George, *Recollections of a New York Chief of Police,* 1887, reprint Patterson Smith & Co., 1972.

Wellman, Francis L., *Luck and Opportunity the Recollections of Francis L. Wellman,* McMillan Comp., 1938.

Willis, Clint, editor, *Crimes of New York,* Thunder Mouth Press, 2003.

NEWSPAPERS AND MAGAZINES:

The Atlanta Constitution, The Bismark Daily Tribune, The Bluefield Daily Telegraph, The Boston Daily Globe, The Brooklyn Eagle, The Daily Continent, The Daily Northwestern, The Halifax Morning Herald, The London Sun, The Manitoba Free Press, The Mountain Democrat, The New York Herald, The New York Sun, The New York Times, The New York Tribune, The Olean Democrat, The Philadelphia Press, The Reno Evening Gazette, The Saint John Globe, The Sandusky Star, The Stevens Point Daily Journal, The Toronto Globe and Mail, The Trenton Times, The Western Queens Gazette, The World

Ripperana:
October 1993,
No. 34, October 2000. "A Tale of Two Frenchy's," Michael Conlon,

Ripperologist:
No. 32, December, 2001, "The Ripper in America," Michael Conlon.
No. 46, May, 2003, "The Carrie Brown Murder Case: New Revelations," Michael Conlon.
No. 48, August 2003, "The Jamaican Jack the Ripper," Stephen Ryder. "Ripper Redux," Michael Conlon.

The Lancet 29 September, 1888.

WEBSITES:

Casebook: Jack the Ripper
www.casebook.org
Barbee, Larry, "An Investigation into the Carrie Brown Murder," dissertation.
"Carrie Brown," victim's profile.

New York Press: nypress.com
Bryk, William, "Inspector Byrnes," news and columns.

The Irish in New York:
www.irishinnyc.freeservers.com

Inspector Thomas Byrnes:
www.library.yale.edu/~mtheroux/19c/19sam4.htm

Jack the Ripper and Technology:
Ripperology in the Twenty-First Century

By John Hacker

*This is software engineer **John Hacker**'s first article
for **Ripper Notes**.*

Maybe it's my avid interest in science fiction, but in a strange way Jack and technology have always been inexorably linked in my mind. Some of my fondest childhood memories were of Scotty on *Star Trek* being possessed by Jack the Ripper in "Wolf in the Fold," of H.G. Welles chasing David Warner to 1980's San Francisco in *Time After Time*, or Jack being pulled into the far future in Harlan Ellison's "The Prowler in the City at the Edge of the World."

Most fascinating of all were those stories where Jack was brought back to life via technology, as Sir William Gull was resurrected in Phillip Jose Farmer's *Riverworld* series to be confronted by his also restored victims.

Fortunately, technology will never bring Jack back. But it can help us come closer to understanding him, the time in which he lived, and the pervasive effect he has had on our culture.

There have been many technological advances between 1888 and today to say the very least. The simplest are perhaps the most important from a humanitarian point of view. Electricity and street lighting are commonplace. We have refrigeration to help preserve our food. Long distance transportation is possible for all but the poorest. Advanced healthcare will preserve our lives far beyond what could have been expected

John Hacker at the Ripper Conference. This article is adapted from his presentation there.

Photo copyright 2004 by Ally Reinecke and Stephen Ryder

then. Telecommunications and satellite technology allow for almost instant communication to virtually anywhere on the planet. Even what are considered the most commonplace and basic technologies today, such as watches, were beyond the reach of most denizens of Whitechapel in 1888.

However I believe it is the changes in information technology that will have the most profound effect upon our society and Ripperology as well. The newly literate population of England feasted upon news of Jack in its newspapers, giving birth to an almost mythical figure. Now our society receives our news via the Internet and television. We can search the Internet for information on almost any subject, and we can see events as they happen almost anywhere in the world. This ready availability of information cannot help but change how we view ourselves in relation to our world or any event or subject we choose to examine in detail.

As technology in general has advanced by leaps and bounds, so has the technology of forensics. Unfortunately, many of the advances we take for granted, such as fingerprinting, profiling and DNA testing, were unknown at the time of the Whitechapel killings. Murders such as those committed by the Ripper are no longer unknown to us, but are commonplace, and their investigation follows well-established protocols.

However, as recent history has clearly shown, forensics is only is good as the evidence available, and, unfortunately, there is no physical evidence that can be tied directly to Jack himself. Despite the investment of millions of dollars and the inversion of the normal investigative process where evidence leads to suspect instead of vice versa, Patricia Cornwell was unable to build a case against Walter Sickert that was much more compelling than that of Jean Overton Fuller, who spent — and made — considerably less.

This is not to say that there is no potential for forensics to aid in the study of Jack the Ripper, however it will require new evidence coming to light that we can apply it to. The most likely scenarios that I can think of would require the exhumation of the victim's bodies, which are the only physical objects we could tie directly to Jack.

There is the potential for forensic reconstruction on Mary Jane Kelly's skull to give her a face, or to restore Catherine Eddowes to give us a better idea of how she would have looked when alive. The recentlly discovered photograph of Annie Chapman while alive was extremely moving, and to see Mary Jane as she might have looked would certainly be a very powerful image and a far cry from the horrific one that is the only pictorial record we have of her.

If we were ever to come across a suspect we could tie to a specific potential murder weapon, it might be possible to compare marks on the victim's skeletons to the weapon to see if there is a match. Admittedly, this is highly unlikely, as any knife that old would likely have been sharpened many times, and its characteristics changed. Or alternatively, its condition would have deteriorated through neglect and the same problem would exist. In any case, the chances of tying any weapon to a known owner at this late date are remote in the extreme.

But if forensics cannot help us, the question becomes "What **can** technology do for us?" The answer, in my opinion, is that the future is in data and computers.

Computational devices are not new. Mechanical computers have existed since the 1600s. In 1965 Gordon Moore predicted that the number of transistors contained on a computer chip would double every year. This has been fairly accurate. The number of transistors and computational speed of new computer chips currently doubles approximately every 18 months. Components continue to shrink in size and grow in speed at an incredible rate.

Law Enforcement Use of Data Processing

The ability of computers to aid in searching through data has been a great help to modern law enforcement.

In 1975 during the search for Ted Bundy a computer program was employed in an attempt to sort through all of the information that they had acquired. They compiled more than 30 lists of names, with more than 300,000 total names. The lists were of people who met certain criteria that they felt might match those of the killer, such as classmates of the initial victim, VW owners, and campus vendors. Taking a week to respond to each request, the computer sorted through the data and produced a list of names that appeared on more than one list. The first attempt produced 1,870 names that appeared on at least two lists, far too many to investigate deeply. The second attempt produced a smaller list of 622 people who appeared on three or more lists. The third and final attempt produced a workable list of 25 names that appeared on 4 or more lists. Ted Bundy's name was on that list. He was, in fact, already on their list of top 100 suspects. It was a week later that Bundy was pulled over in Utah and immediately became the focus of the investigation.

Today computers are much faster, of course, and law enforcement has access to a number of specialized databases to match fingerprints and DNA samples. Killings can be matched to similar killings in other areas, helping to identify serial killers who kill in multiple jurisdictions. The search for terrorists after the 9/11 terrorist attacks has led to databases of incredible size with information about ordinary citizens. Their bank transactions, and associations are used to sift out any potential terrorists, a prospect that I, quite frankly, find a little terrifying.

However, as powerful and potentially useful as these advances are, their application in the study of historical crimes such as those of the Whitechapel killer are extremely limited. So the question becomes, what can technology do for us? How is it being used currently, and what does the future hold?

There are five main areas that I believe technology can benefit us. These are the dissemination of information, research, collaboration, data archiving, and more effective presentation of the information that we do have to make it more accessible.

Where are we now?

Technology has already begun to have a major impact on Ripperology. Let's take a quick look at where we are today in terms of the use of technology in regards to Jack the Ripper, and what the advantages and disadvantages are.

The ready dissemination of information is probably the area that is most apparent to most non-Ripperologists. Patricia Cornwell's ready access to television talk shows helped popularize the unlikely notion that Walter Sickert committed the Whitechapel killings, but it also brought the killings back into the public eye in a way not seen since the Maybrick Diary of the early '90s. The movie *From Hell,* although wildly inaccurate in many ways, conveyed the look and feel of Whitechapel in a manner that was more compelling than the dry narratives of most factual Ripper books, bringing the city to life, if not the historical figures within it.

Unfortunately however, while books and movies such as these that become the most popular do raise awareness of the crimes, and most impart some factual information, they create any number of false impressions in the general public that take years to dispel. Sadly, it's still not unusual to run into people who believe that Sir William Gull killed five women to cover up a royal indiscretion.

On the research front we fare somewhat better. More and more information is becoming available in electronic format. Perhaps most significantly, the census information is being entered into databases, allowing easy searching for specific people and residents of a street or area. With luck, prison, hospital, and travel records will eventually follow suit.

The potential inherent in this form of research is immense. Eventually we may be able to provide alibis for some of the known suspects in this fashion, or discover new likely candidates based on information un-

covered in this way. Unfortunately, of course, the information in databases is only as good as what is entered into them. And the records of the time were handwritten, so it will always be necessary to go back to the original source whenever possible because there are certain to be errors in transcription.

Of course the holy grail of at-home research is the Internet. It makes accessing information on virtually any subject a relatively simple prospect. (Not to mention offering exciting investment opportunities, potency enhancing pills, and any number of other scams through the miracle of spam.) Using search engines such as Google or Yahoo it is possible to find websites on virtually any subject. Much of the information is wildly inaccurate of course, but a lot of research can be done without ever leaving your chair.

Websites exist to service almost any hobby or interest. The complete texts of tens of thousands of books are available. There are message boards and chat rooms where you can meet up with knowledgeable folks on virtually any subject and try to get assistance with any specific questions you might have. Genealogical research is, in many cases, easily accomplished through a quick entry in a search engine.

While researching various Ripper related topics, I've dug up information on such diverse subjects as Victorian history and fashions, the laws of England and the practices of London's police and its prostitutes. I've delved into the histories of several of the suspects. I've looked up medical information regarding the rate of human digestion, methods for estimating the time of death, and the ease of kidney removal. I've even dug into scientific areas such as the melting point of tin, the chemical composition of Victorian inks, and the rate of oxidation of brass.

Just a few short years ago, research of this kind would have required extensive trips to various libraries and long hours of pouring through hundreds if not thousands of books. Now I can do comprehensive research while sitting at my desk, wearing a robe and scarfing chips, chugging Mountain Dew while blaring Offspring's "Americana" at 11 on the volume knob without fear of a librarian telling me to "Shush." Now that's progress!

However there is a downside to the researching on the Internet of course, and that is that there is no guarantee that any information you find is accurate. Many websites provide inaccurate information or information that is slanted to a particular point of view. However this is a problem with printed books as well. In particular, I have shelves of books on Jack himself that are full of misinformation and the twisting of facts to support a theory. At least with the Internet it is possible to access multiple sources quickly to confirm your findings, or at least to gain a balanced perspective.

Perhaps even more important than research, however, is the potential the Internet brings for collaboration and the sharing of information and perspectives between those with similar interests. And there can be little doubt that the single greatest collaborative asset available to Ripperologists is the website, *Casebook: Jack the Ripper* (www.casebook.org). In fact, I will go a step farther and say that, in my opinion, the *Casebook* is the single greatest technological aid that Ripperology currently has at its disposal.

The *Casebook* offers many resources for the casual, as well as the serious, student of the case. There is a good primer on the case for the novice written by Larry Barbee. There are overviews of the victims, both canonical and speculative, as well as the police officials, witnesses, and a great many of the named suspects. There is a detailed timeline of the crimes, copies of several of the more significant Ripper letters, and even a number of interactive games.

For those with a more serious interest, there are official documents, including parliamentary debates. There is extensive background material on London, with more than 40 articles on Whitechapel, Victorian London, and the history of the city itself. There are also dozens of dissertations on various aspects of the case, some reprinted from *Ripper Notes* or *Ripperologist*, while others are original.

Of significant interest, there are

hundreds of press reports from more than 200 different newspapers from a dozen different countries. This allows the user to gain a perspective on how the crimes were seen worldwide in a way that would have previously been difficult if not impossible without incredibly extensive research. These articles, transcribed by hand in many cases by volunteers organized by the late Adrian M. "Viper" Phypers, contain a wealth of information and a much more intimate and visceral look at the case than is available in most of the books on the subject.

There are also the complete texts of several books, including the hard to find *Jack the Myth* by A.P. Wolf, both volumes of the invaluable collections *The First Fifty Years of Jack the Ripper*, and *The Lighter Side of my Official Life* by Sir Robert Anderson. Enough text exists on the *Casebook* to keep the average reader busy for months if not years. There is simply not a more complete repository of information on the case to be found currently.

However it is the collaborative aspects of the *Casebook* that are the most valuable. They have started to change the way that modern Ripperologists work. Previously, Ripperology was a more or less solo sport, with the occasional collaboration between two or three individuals or dueling articles in one of the dedicated periodicals. Now, through the *Casebook* message boards and chat room, people can exchange ideas and information almost in real time.

By allowing users to place messages where all can see them and reply in an organized fashion, the message boards provide a great mechanism for long-term discussion. The nature of the format allows

people to post complex ideas with a great degree of detail at their own pace. And because they are archived, anyone can enter the debate at any point and read through the discussion from the beginning to the most current posts without missing anything.

The message boards provide a wonderful forum for running debate, allowing would be authors to test their ideas on a well informed and skeptical audience before committing their words to paper. People new to the case can ask questions and get the opinions of any number of regular posters with completely different perspectives on the same issue. It's also a great place to meet people with similar interests, enabling them sharing of information and pooling of efforts and resources to work on an independent project. And of course they offer the unparalleled opportunity to go round in circles with the same cast of characters for literally years over minutia that your spouse or significant other would roll his or her eyes at the very mention of.

> I call it the "Bloody Raving Loonies" problem, and it too isn't going away soon.

For those who prefer a more rapid and conversational approach, there is the chat room. This is a less public forum that only those in the room at the time can participate in, allowing for more intimate discussions and a much quicker exchange of ideas. It's the place that desperate high school students turn up in at 10 p.m. with a paper due the next day, unwilling to hear that Sir William Gull probably wasn't the killer and that Abberline was not, in fact, an opium addict.

By raising awareness of new information as it becomes available and putting vast amounts of information at the disposal of its users, the *Casebook* website brings armchair

Ripperology into the reach of everyone. And by promoting public discussion on new books and theories, those who are interested in the facts of the case can get an alternate perspective on the theory of the week, which might not change their minds but will certainly give them more information to base their opinion upon.

Of course there are downsides to such worldwide collaboration. There is an engineering term called "Signal to Noise Ratio." When very little of the signal is noise, it's a good thing. However sometimes there's an awful lot of static in that signal and the ratio goes all to hell. The same sort of thing can happen on forums. Quite often a discussion will devolve to the point that there is no longer any useful information being conveyed, yet for some reason it goes on and on anyhow. This happens in all unmoderated discussions everywhere and can always be expected. You just have to learn to tune it out. The other downside is one that has plagued Ripperology for quite some time now. I call it the "Bloody Raving Loonies" problem, and it too isn't going away soon.

One of the true tragedies of the Jack the Ripper case from a historical perspective is the amount of information that has been lost. Most of the original case files are gone and will never be recovered. What we have to work with now is only a small subset of what the police officials of 1888 had at their disposal. Fortunately, technology can help make sure that this doesn't happen in the future. Today's technology makes the storage of vast amounts of data practical and secure. For example, the entire *Casebook:* *Jack the Ripper* website is available on CD-ROM. It contains copies of innumerable newspapers and source files, as well as its message boards, pictures and text.

Presentation is an area in which technology has great potential, but so far we have barely scratched the surface, with a few notable exceptions (many of them of them from the *Casebook*). One of the most interesting has been the ongoing analysis of the crime scene photos from Miller's Court. There has been any number of threads on the *Casebook* message boards through the years in which various enhancements have been made to the photographs, trying to make sense of the horrible Picasso-like puzzle that has been left to us. The photographs have been colorized, divided by grid, retouched, and sketched over.

In the past, this sort of work would be difficult and require great artistic skills, but today, working with modern and readily available photo enhancement software, that work is within the reach of the everyday user regardless of their native skill.

Another use that has popped up from time to time are various 3-D renderings of Mary Kelly's room, detailed to show the relationship between the various articles of furniture and the doors and window. They allow us to see the room from points of view other than the two static photos that we have. By looking at the room from different angles, we can get a better insight into how events might have transpired.

Technology also played an integral part in rebuilding Whitechapel for the film *From Hell*. Many of the shots used computer graphics to recreate various landmarks of London. Christchurch, as shown in the film, was physically built only at the bottom, while computer imaging created the upper portions.

One of the most creative uses I have seen for using technology to present information in an interesting way was a website that was apparently intended at one time to promote a movie about the Maybrick Diary. It allowed the user to chat with Jack the Ripper, and, by analyzing the user's input, it would attempt to respond with an appropriate quote from the diary text. It didn't carry on a particularly coherent conversation, but then the diary wasn't a very coherent document. The same site also allowed you to chat with John Lennon.

While technology allows the creation of incredibly detailed images and 3-D models, as well as many other engaging forms of presentation, the downside is that the actual source information is not as detailed as we like. So in some cases we need to rely on assumptions. But the end result is only as good as the assumptions that went into it, no matter how compelling the end result is. Computer programmers have an expression that pretty well sums it up: "Garbage in, Garbage out."

The question remains, where can we go from here? The reality of technology will probably never reach the levels suggested in science fiction, which is unfortunate. So I've put together a list of the top five things technology should do for Ripperology but won't:

#5: WCTV: Whitechapel television, on Pay-per-View: The ultimate in reality television.

#4: The Retro Polygraph: A lie detector for evaluating the witness statements.

#3: The Necrophone: A telephone for speaking to the dead, so we could ask the important questions.

#2: A Delusion Detector: A device that Ripperologists could wear on their heads to tell when they're fooling themselves, even if they're not fooling anyone else.

And the #1 thing that technology won't give us that it should: Closure on the Diary.

Of the five areas I originally described — dissemination of information, data archiving, research, collaboration, and presentation — I think that the dissemilnation of information is the area that will change the least in terms of effectiveness. It will all come down to getting information out to two basic audiences: the general public and the Ripperologists. Ripperologists will always have some form of specialty communications network, as exists with most hobbies, be it magazine, email, Internet site or some new form of communication. Reaching the general public, however, will always depend on some form of sensationalism. It might be in 3-D with surround sound and smell-o-vision, but it will still be Cornwell or Knight at its heart: entertaining perhaps, but probably not educational.

Research is an area that will advance in leaps and bounds through the years to come. More information will become availlable online. More newspapers, archival records and census reports will be easily referenced as they are eventually migrated to electronic storage. In particular, as research into genealogies is pooled, we should be able to track the principal players, their descendants, and their ancestors much more easily. As standards emerge for the storage of various types of data, it will be much easier to search through these various sources without having to learn each system individually.

The searching of these combined data sources will be made much easier as search engines improve. Today, we use text based sites such as Yahoo, Alta Vista, and Google to search the Internet. These engines look through their databases to find websites that contain the words you specify. Unfortunately today, you're just as likely to find a creatively marketed pornographic site as one with actual research value. But improvements in fuzzy logic systems and natural language processing will eventually

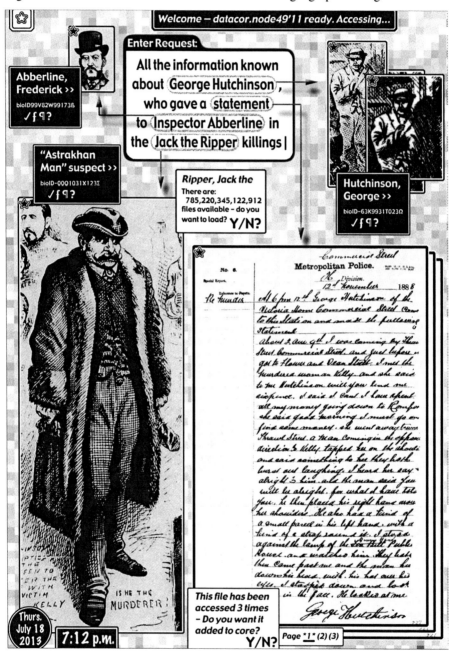

allow us to search based on specific criteria that is entered in a much more natural fashion. It will be years before we get there, but eventually we will reach the point where we should be able to ask the public network to give us "all information known about George Hutchinson, who gave a statement to Inspector Abberline in the Jack the Ripper killings" and then get all of the newspaper articles, his census records, his birth and death certificates, as well as any the text of any books that reference him.

One appealing possibility is that much of the East End probably exists in unlabeled photographs. It is entirely possible that someday all of the available photographs and maps could be scanned into computers, and, using advanced image recognition and A.I. routines, they could be identified and joined together where possible to create a much more complete picture of how the area actually looked than we can from the few identified photos we now have access to. In fact, the technology exists today to allow you to take a digital photo of where you are and have a service identify your position and direct you where you want to go.

Collaboration is an area that will improve greatly in ease of use and accessibility, but its functionality probably won't grow too far beyond what is currently technologically possible. Today we have all of the functionality provided by the *Casebook*. Also available, but much less used, are programs that allow face to face video conferencing, the sharing of photos and sound files, and interactive whiteboards with which people can sketch their points. This sort of functionality will become more accessible with time, and it will become more immersive. Virtual reality headsets are already available, and it's not too much of a stretch to imagine that at some point the chat rooms of the future will allow people to interact as 3-D avatars of themselves, or that the message boards might be available as animated videos of the posters speaking.

Data archiving is primarily a matter of scale and reliability. It will become more secure and capable of higher degrees of data storage. To give you an idea of how much we have progressed, a disc from my first personal computer from 20 years ago could hold approximately 128,000 bytes of information. A DVD-ROM from my current system can hold 4.7 gigabytes, or approximately 37 million times as much information.

In addition, newer media such as CDs and DVD-ROMs are much more secure and dependable than older magnetic media like floppy discs, which are subject to erasure from magnets or close proximity to monitors. Barring physical damage, the data on these discs should remain safe and intact for many years to come. And with the increasing importance of the Internet, there is redundancy in storage. Most information available on the Web can be found in multiple locations, so even if one of them should encounter some form of disaster, the information available on it need not necessarily be lost.

The enhanced presentation of information is another area that future technological advances should greatly aid. Computers have become very good at generating realistic environments in real time, and will only become more powerful in the future. Given enough maps, photographs, building records, and time, it would be possible to create a reasonably accurate virtual reality representation of Whitechapel as it existed in 1888. Wouldn't it be incredible to go on a guided "Walking Tour" in a 3-D Whitechapel populated by realistic virtual inhabitants, with no cars and all of the sites intact? We will never have enough data to make a perfect replica of course, but one that accurately conveys the street layout, style of architecture and style of dress and is illuminated by period lighting is entirely possible.

In a similar vein, interactive maps could be produced that utilized census data. You could select any address and see who was living there, and look up and down each street scanning the inhabitants. Or you could search for a name and see where everyone with that name lived. You could even have it automatically draw the shortest route between two points, like the maps on Yahoo today.

I've described in fairly broad terms some of the potential available for the use of technology to advance Ripperology, but I would like to go into a bit more depth with one specific example that touches on both presentation and collaboration. It's what I like to call the A-Z of the future.

I am sure that many readers have copies of The Jack the Ripper A-Z by Paul Begg, Martin Fido, and Keith Skinner, and The Complete Jack the Ripper Companion by Stewart Evans and Keith Skinner. They are both invaluable tools, and I recommend them highly to anyone with an interest in the case. The A-Z presents information about the various people, places, and events in an encyclopedic fashion. The Companion, on the other hand, provides transcriptions of actual police, inquest, and news reports, providing primary source evidence.

However they are both limited in a way. The A-Z presents information in an accessible fashion, but it generally doesn't provide any form of link or reference to the source material that the entries are derived

from. The Companion provides a great deal of source material, but it is much less accessible than the A-Z. Both are constrained by limitations on the size of a published work and by the amount of work that two or three authors can put into a book. In addition, a book is a static thing. Once it's finished, it's no longer updated as new information becomes available. These are the sorts of problems that technology can handle for us very well.

So what would the A-Z of the future be like? Ideally, what we would have is an online, collaborative system that allow individuals to contribute information, that references the source material directly, and presents the information to users in a way that is clear, accessible, and easy to navigate between related items. Of course, allowing individuals to contribute information would be a double-edged sword. More information would get into the system, but there is no guarantee that it would be accurate.

For such a system to be reliable there would need to be a method in place to ensure the reliability of data. All information submitted would need a source reference and verification by a team of human volunteers before being allowed into the main system. All source material would also need to be transcribed, entered, and verified in a similar fashion.

As far as entering and storing the many diverse pieces of information related to the Jack the Ripper case, there are many possibilities, but whatever solution is used should be extensible so that new types of information can be added as it becomes necessary. It must also be capable of handling multiple values for each piece of information because the all of the sources are not in agreement. The amount of data collected should be as complete as possible for every person, place, or event that is recorded. For example a person would have data such as name, birth date, occupations, a list of known addresses and the dates lived at each, height, hair color, and anything else that might apply to a given person. Depending on their specific relevance to the case, they might also have police, suspect, or witness data with more specific information that would apply.

Using a system like this would have several advantages. It would give a standardized format to keep and display all data. It also would give us something to shoot for in terms of gathering available information to fill in as many of the blanks as possible for each person, place, or event. Each piece of data would also record the source or sources and the people who entered and verified the data. By recording the source, people would be able to make up their own minds as to how much weight to assign a given piece of information.

In fact, it would be easy to set up the system so that the user could filter out all information from sources that they flag as unreliable or to show only the information provided by a single source. This degree of control over the information presented would allow the user to see at a glance what facts were reported in the Times, or what specific pieces of information were provided by Mrs. Maxwell's testimony.

Most importantly, the information would be linked between people, places, and events. For example, a user could surf through the data from Mary Jane Kelly, to Joe Barnett, to the inquest testimony, to Dr. Bond, to the post mortem, and back to Mary Jane Kelly. This would allow users to explore the case in any fashion they liked, check sources and follow up on any details or related matters that should cross their minds.

The technology exists to do this today. All it would require is server access, some dedicated programmer time, and willing volunteers to help maintain it. I've actually started some preliminary work in this direction, however putting all the pieces together and actually building a complete and usable A-Z in this fashion would take years of people contributing their time and dedication into filling it with data. I don't know if we'll ever get there, but in the meantime it's a nice dream.

> **Maybe a super-computer with a powerful A.I. program will scan through the case data and historical records and be able to tell us with a 99.9% probability who Jack was.**

Advances in technology will enhance all aspects of our society and will certainly transform the way we live and work. I'm not Nostradamus. I cannot see into the future. All of the possibilities I have prolposed are based on existing technology and looking at how it could be applied as it becomes more powerful and easier to use. There will certainly be advances that we cannot currently imagine that may overlshadow everything that came before. Perlhaps in 20 or 30 years time a physicist will invent a "rear view mirror" that we could tote around to the crime scenes to see what occurred there in 1888. Maybe a super-computer with a powerful A.I. program will scan through the case data and historical records and be able to tell us with a 99.9% probability who Jack was. In any case, the future will certainly hold some very interesting surprises.

But let us keep in mind that technological advances will be useful to all areas of research and in any subject that there is a sufficiently interested community to exploit them. There will be resources dedicated to Victorian London, medical research, criminal psychiatry, crime in general, and countless other subjects that will greatly benefit our research. And our work will in some way contribute to theirs.

Universities in particular are likely to become high tech information centers as the many hard to find academic books and other rare tomes are finally put into electronic format for preservation, ease of access, and the ability to search through them. This will make available information and ideas that, even with today's Internet, we cannot now easily access.

One thing I feel quite safe in saying is that in the future technology will be far more accessible than it is today. Historically, devices have always become easier to use with time. With the massive advances in computer technology of late, many of the more powerful functions are arcane and difficult to use. However, some of the features that are now easy to use, such as digital photography and editing, movie making, web searching, and word processing were once exceedingly difficult. In particular, the predecessors of today's word processors were exceedingly difficult to install and use. 20 years ago I was able to make a good living charging 200 dollars an hour to install and configure Word Perfect on IBM PCs. Today installing, configuring, and using a word processing program is a simple operation. With time, the functionality that is difficult today will become easier to use, and the more people adopt the newer technologies, the greater the impetus will be for others to use them.

In addition, the generations that follow us are growing up with the new technologies, so we're literally coming at this from two different angles. Not only will the techlnology be easier to use, we're raising a generation of children that will find all of these things to be natural and instinctive. Our children will be able to do truly amazing things with the tools that techlnollogy will provide them. Unfortulnately, having grown up with them, they won't realize just how amazing they are, in the same way that we take cars, television, radio, and refrigeration for granted.

This brings up interesting questions. What will the next generation of Ripperologists be like? What will their focus be, and how will they work?

They will certainly have advantages over those who came before them. After all, they have more than 100 years of mistakes and silly theories to learn from. They will also have access to more complete information, and it will be much more accessible than it was to those who pioneered the field by pawing through boxes of old records and pouring over 100 year old newspapers looking for a small piece of new information.

But will they learn from the mistakes of the past and throw out wild speculation and sensationalism in favor of a more academic approach that contributes to our overall understanding of the case? It will undoubtedly depend on the individual. There will always be those who for some reason or other are drawn to wild speculation and are utterly convinced by their own theories. In fact, it's entirely possible that the ease of research will make this more prevalent. As more information is uncovlered, the easier it will be to build a circumlstantial case against John Q. Suspect. And with less time needed for research, that leaves all that much more time for speculation.

As with most things, it will depend on the individuals. But whatever their inclination is — speculation, historical research, the social impact of Jack the Ripper on Victorian London, or his effect on popular culture — they will have more information, and better tools to pursue their interest as they choose.

They will certainly be better informed and equipped, but this won't make them better Ripperologists. The true giants of the field had to go and dig through moldy old newspapers and case files doing their own research, relentlessly tracking down leads and bits of information. The next generation of Ripperologists will have a treasure trove of information at their disposal, but it will be due in large part to people like Donald Rumbelow, Stewart Evans and Phillip Sugden, whose research was due to hard work and dedication, and without whom many of us would never have developed such a deep interest in a century old murder case.

Speaking of the Internet, did you know that *Ripper Notes* has a website?

It's brand new! You can subscribe or renew your subscription using a credit card, learn what we have planned for upcoming issues, and read online copies of old articles.

Just point your browser at:

www.RipperNotes.com

or

www.Ripperology.com

Web hosting provided by www.HostIdea.com

The Strange Case of Dr. John Hewitt

By Stan Russo

*Stan Russo is the author of the soon to be released **The Jack the Ripper Suspects: Persons Cited by Investigators and Theorists,** published by McFarland & Co. It can be ordered through* www.mcfarlandpub.com *or participating bookstores.*

In 1985 an accountant named Steward Hicks proposed an entirely new suspect for the murderer popularly known as Jack the Ripper. After discovering his name in the records of the Lunacy Commission in London, Hicks relayed his new idea to legendary true crime historian Colin Wilson, who had become a self proclaimed "clearing house" for theories on the case. Hicks recalled the story told by Sir Osbert Sitwell, in 1947 and again in 1950, of a young veterinary student who aroused the suspicion of his landlady due to his obsession with the murders during the time they were committed. Hicks believed he had identified this young veterinary student as Dr. John Hewitt, born in 1850, who died in 1892 of a general paralysis of the insane. With this interesting new discovery Hicks wholeheartedly believed he had found the murderer, and Wilson was incredibly optimistic about his findings.

This infamous young veterinary student, described by Osbert Sitwell, is attributed to the Victorian painter Walter Sickert. Sickert stated that the landlady of this student told him the information directly upon Sickert renting the same room. This information included that this student would stay out all night on specific occasions, then rush to buy the earliest edition of the morning papers to read about the murders. This young man also burnt the clothes he was wearing on these nights. The student was frail, perhaps inflicted with consumption, and in ill health. Shortly after the murders ceased his widowed mother

Stan Russo looks over his notes at the Ripper Conference. This article is an expanded version of the presentation he gave there.

Photo copyright 2004 by Ally Reinecke and Stephen Ryder

took him home to Bournemouth, where he passed away three months later. This is the story Sickert relayed to Sitwell and is now a matter of public record in connection with the case.

Hewitt, identified by Hicks as Sickert and Sitwell's veterinary student, is a fascinating suspect, complete with a number of bizarre mitigating factors surrounding his distinctive situation. He fits the major believed mindset of what the murderer must have been: a loner, without any ties to impede his murderous lust, suffering from some form of insanity and having a specific reason explaining why the murders must have ceased, in this case his having moved to Bournemouth shortly after the killings ended. Hewitt also fit the broad characteristics of what was reported about Sickert's young veterinary student, with only minor differences. However, it was his name, as opposed to his true viability as a candidate, that eventually brought Hewitt into the suspect pool, and that is where the story becomes even more intriguing.

But as absorbing as the circumstances surrounding Hewitt are, enough about him for right now though.

What defines a person as a suspect? Unfortunately there is no standard definition. Over the years, as the case has evolved, a suspect's candidacy has generally remained consistent. The primary basis for any person becoming a suspect is proposal. Without proposal, in fact, there would be no suspects. While there is no general rating scale regarding suspects to determine actual viability, many suspects rank or rate higher than others, purely from an academic standpoint. Key examples of this are that Montague John Druitt is a far likelier suspect than Lewis Carroll, and Aaron Kosminski is much more of a candidate than Joseph Fleming. In the academic community Druitt and Kosminski are generally considered primary suspects while Carroll and Fleming — as well as numerous others such as John McCarthy, Dr. Jon William Sanders, Frederick Nicholas Charrington and the Norwegian sailor Fogelma — are often referred to as the laughable suspects, considered by many as a waste of time and valuable research effort. One question immediately comes to mind regarding this philosophy: Why?

All of the above individuals have been proposed as the murderer, with numerous others included in that distinct group. Why the difference in opinion from one suspect to the next? There is no evidence linking anyone to the murders. This is perhaps one of the most important statements in connection with this murder case, so I shall repeat it. There is no evidence linking anyone to the murders. I must state that I am not the first researcher or theorist to make this claim in print, and this principle has now become commonplace within the field.

Why then are certain suspects viewed with a higher degree of disdain or, more to the point, an elevated laughable quotient? It appears that the way a suspect is proposed, mainly the theory of why that suspect committed the murders, is directly responsible for shaping the minds of the academic community. In fact it is more than just the mere appearance of specific suspect partiality, it is obvious that a non-malicious bias exists against certain suspects. Let's try to examine why.

The two suspects mentioned above in the category of, to nicely put it, extremely unlikely, Carroll and Fleming, were first proposed during the late 20th century. It is, however, their unique proposal that has earned these suspects, and many more like them, a relatively diminished status within the case.

The children's author Lewis Carroll, born Charles Lutwidge Dodgson, was first proposed as the murderer in a 1996 book written by theorist Richard Wallace. Wallace's argument, or theory, revolves around his belief that Carroll was a pedophile who displayed extreme signs of deranged psychopathology. His theory of why the murders were committed is a convoluted mish-mash of numbers games revolving around the number 42 and Carroll's own inner demons suppressed by the prim and proper Victorian era. Wallace even mentions an accomplice, Carroll's friend Thomas Vere Bayne. The theory set forth by Wallace of why Lewis Carroll committed the murders is laughable, therefore his suspect is also deemed as such.

The suspect Joseph Fleming was first proposed in the early 1990s by researcher Mark King. He discovered that a lunatic named Joseph Fleming had died in Claybury Mental Hospital in 1920. This Joseph Fleming, also known as James Evans, has never been proved to be the Joseph Fleming that Mary Kelly knew, who might have visited her in and around the time of her murder. Even King states that precaution should be taken, only suggesting that, if the two Joseph Flemings were the same person, then he should be examined as a possible suspect due to the fact that he died in a mental hospital. Distinctly less than a theory, King's suggestion is nothing more than a researcher exhausting every possible outlet, and his finds are important. With as little as is currently known about the mason or plasterer Joseph Fleming, he is widely considered as a non-suspect, despite the doubts and possibilities raised under the flag of exhaustive academic research.

Of the above two named individuals, there is a non-suspect and a laughable suspect. Both have a major element in common, despite their varying degrees of believability: the theories regarding their suspect candidacy are wholly unconvincing. In this setting, to convert a suspect to laughable status or propose a new suspect and create laughable status, only requires a wholly unconvincing theory regarding that suspect. This is much easier done than said. What is not reflected in this instance is the possibility that, outside of these unconvincing theories, the suspect actually could have committed the murders. Why then are two primary suspects, Druitt and Kosminski, still treated differently from Carroll and Fleming? It is not entirely because of the theories surrounding their candidacy. It has more to do with the impeccable sources that are responsible for their proposal, Assistant Chief Constable Melville Macnaghten and Assistant Commissioner Robert Anderson, respectively.

In 1894 Macnaghten wrote a confidential report to refute the claims of a magazine titled *The Sun*. This magazine claimed that the murderer was Thomas Cutbush, nephew of former superintendent Charles Cutbush. Macnaghten's goal was to refute these claims, so he offered three candidates who were considered more likely than Cutbush to have committed the murders. There are three drafts of this report, known as the Macnaghten Memorandum, and there is no doubt as to whom Macnaghten's preferred

suspect was, the only suspect mentioned in all three versions: Montague John Druitt.

Macnaghten's theory about the man responsible for the Autumn of Terror in 1888 is that the killer's brain gave way after committing the horrific murder in Miller's Court and that he committed suicide. Macnaghten does offer an alternate, what he believed was a less likely version: that the murderer was confined to an asylum after his relatives found him insane. Macnaghten later adds that he believed the killer was at one time at the bottom of the Thames River, displaying his ardent belief in Druitt's guilt. In the suspect section on Druitt, right after the above statement, Macnaghten states that Druitt disappeared at the time of the Miller's Court murder. Macnaghten also claimed Druitt was a doctor and that he was about 41 years of age. These conclusions on the part of Macnaghten are the crux of his belief in Druitt's guilt.

Druitt, however, did not disappear at the time of the Miller's Court murder on November 9th. He continued his duties as both an assistant headmaster and barrister, acting as special pleader in an appeal of a voter registration case on November 22nd. Druitt also attended his monthly meeting of the Blackheath Football, Cricket and Lawn Tennis Company on November 19th, acting as Honorary Secretary and Treasurer, a post he had held since 1885. Druitt was definitively not in hiding nor had he disappeared immediately after November 9th. Macnaghten also believed Druitt was a doctor. He was not. Macnaghten stated Druitt's age as 41. He was only 31. In fact, in Macnaghten's earliest draft he even gets Druitt's first name wrong, identifying him as Michael. These are the major elements of Macnaghten's theory or belief in the guilt of Montague John Druitt. All of the above elements have been shown as erroneous, yet Druitt still remains as a primary suspect today. Even those devoted Druittites, abundant in the 1960s and 1970s, have seriously decreased in numbers.

Macnaghten was around during the time of the murders, but was he an impeccable source? Hardly. He never worked one minute of any murder case in 1888. For those who do not know, Macnaghten did not join the force until June 1889. The murder of Alice McKenzie, originally investigated as part of the same case file, occurred the month after Macnaghten assumed his post, and yet few if any reports mention Macnaghten as actively taking part in the investigation.

one. I may mention the cases of 3 men, any one of whom would have been more likely than Cutbush to have committed this series of murders:-

(1) A Mr M.J. Druitt, said to be a doctor or of good family - who disappeared at the time of the Miller's Court murder, whose body (which was said to have been upwards of a month in the water) was found in the Thames on 31st Dec. - or about 7 weeks after that murder. He was sexually insane and from private info I have little doubt but that his own family believed him to have been the murderer.

(2) Kosminski - a Polish Jew & resident in Whitechapel. This man became insane owing to many years indulgence in solitary vices. He had a great hatred of women, specially of the prostitute class, & had strong homicidal tendencies; he was removed to a lunatic asylum about March 1889. There were many circs connected with this man which made him a strong "suspect".

(3) Michael Ostrog, a Russian doctor, and a convict, who was subsequently detained in a lunatic asylum as a homicidal maniac. This man's antecedents were of the worst possible type, and his whereabouts at the time of the murders could never be ascertained.

The Macnaghten Memorandum names three suspects: M.J. Druitt, Kosminski and Michael Ostrog.

Former Commissioner Charles Warren described Macnaghten as incompetent and blocked his original appointment in 1887. Chief Inspector Donald Swanson described Macnaghten as annoying Anderson regarding a threatening letter related to the case. Even James Monro, the man who originally offered the post to Macnaghten in 1887, chose another man for the vacated post of Chief Constable after Warren had resigned and could not block the appointment further. Macnaghten was originally intended to serve as Assistant Chief Constable and then move up to Chief Constable upon the retirement of Adolphus Williamson. Even without Warren as an impediment, Monro chose not to appoint Macnaghten to a post he was originally intended to take over. This to me shows that James Monro, Macnaghten's original attempted benefactor, also had serious doubts regarding the level of his competency.

Macnaghten would eventually rise to the position of Assistant Commissioner, but where are the accolades surrounding his career outside his report on these murders? Recollections of Macnaghten are of the general nature that he was a likable guy and held a deep interest in crime. I have not yet found a reminiscence that describes Macnaghten as an exceptional officer who made a major difference in any particular case or event. Macnaghten's impeccability as a reliable source seems highly challengeable in light of the facts of the case and those who knew him. Why does this not affect the status of Montague John Druitt as a suspect?

Kosminski was first mentioned as a suspect in the Macnaghten Memorandum, although his name only appears in two of the three versions. His re-emergence as a suspect occurred in the late 1980s, when he was identified as Robert Anderson's Polish Jew suspect. As such, Kosminski, whether it was Aaron Kosminski or another Kosminski, belongs to Anderson. There is good reason for this, although a return to Macnaghten momentarily must take place.

One of the all important questions of the case that I have not seen answered yet is why Macnaghten was chosen to write the official report to refute the claims that Thomas Cutbush was the murderer. In Macnaghten's earliest draft he names three suspects, Michael John Druitt, a Polish Jew nicknamed Leather Apron and a feeble minded man who stabbed young girls. This last suspect is a direct reference to Thomas Cutbush. The mention of these suspects, the feeble minded man in particular, also dates this earliest draft at some time during 1891. It was during this time when Macnaghten fell out of favor with the CID, but these relations were fixed somehow just prior to having Macnaghten transferred to the uniform branch.

No mention of how Macnaghten repaired his problematic relationship has surfaced, but inferential deduction leads me to believe that his difficulty began because of his constant troublesome nature regarding the murders and that the repairing of this relationship dealt specifically with Macnaghten's original draft of who the three most likely suspects were. This made Mac-

naghten the perfect candidate to write the confidential report that attempted to denounce Thomas Cutbush as a suspect. So how did Kosminski eventually get in there?

The man whom Macnaghten most likely had to repair his relationship with had to be Robert Anderson. And it seems that Robert Anderson is the man who supplied Macnaghten with the suspect Kosminski.

The Swanson Marginalia end notes mention the alleged identification of Kosminski.

From Anderson to Macnaghten, Kosminski becomes the Polish Jew suspect Leather Apron. How could this happen? The original Leather Apron was identified as John Pizer, who was cleared of the murders. The timing plays an important factor. Thomas Cutbush was incarcerated on March 5th, 1891. Kosminski was placed inside Mile End Old Town Workhouse Infirmary almost exactly one month previously, on February 4th, 1891. One of the factors for his incarceration into Colney Hatch Lunatic Asylum was that Kosminski threatened his sister with a knife. A report to the police of this activity would have been standard, especially since there was a belief that the murderer might still be out there. Just one week later Frances Coles was murdered and immediate connections to the original murders sprung up. It would have been the duty of Colney Hatch to inform the authorities of what they had just learned. This is a likely possibility of how Macnaghten's Leather Apron became Kosminski.

As with Macnaghten, the question arises: Was Anderson an impeccable source? That is a serious matter for debate, and a debate that rages on today. There is a definitive division within those who study or research this case, pro-Anderson and anti-Anderson.

There are numerous instances in which Anderson's credibility can be called into question. Anderson anonymously authored articles for *The Times* accusing Irish nationalist Charles Stewart Parnell of having involvement in Fenian terrorism. Parnell was eventually cleared of all charges due to a lack of any shred of evidence. In this aspect, Anderson directly lied about Parnell and as a result forced the removal of an undercover agent working within the Fenian underground movement for more than twenty years. Anderson was discussed in a recent book titled *Fenian Fire,* in which the author, Christy Campbell, portrays an incredibly unflattering picture of him, going so far as to insinuate he was an outright liar. Despite having been born of Irish descent, Anderson worked within the Anti-Fenian movement in England as a spymaster. He was decidedly pro-English and his loyalty was to the Queen above all. As a lifelong spy, or involved in the spy network, just how far his loyalties would have taken Anderson are up for debate. This, however, tarnishes Anderson's unimpeachable presence as an unchallengeable source.

Furthermore, I recently learned from researcher Stephen P. Ryder that within Anderson's papers at Duke University was a document about the questionable activity of one of Anderson's close friends, Sir Thomas Snagge. The document pertained to Snagge stealing a woman's purse and then running away from a police constable. The matter was not taken to the next level, yet it seems apparent that Anderson removed a possibly harmful document from police files to protect the good name of his friend. This, of course, was most likely out of the scope of following police regulations. Anderson was loyal. No one ever argues that fact. It is the extent of Anderson's loyalty that calls his character and credibility into question. Just how far would Anderson have gone in protecting what he believed in? The debate continues and appears headed nowhere.

As a reliable source Anderson is questionable at best, but what of Kosminski?

> More importantly, this implies that Swanson received the name Kosminski directly from Anderson.

Anderson's theory at its most basic form was that Kosminski was a deranged lunatic who murdered these women for the mere pleasure of the kill. The primary belief in Kosminski as a suspect is Anderson's assurance that there was a witness identification of Kosminski. Anderson never reveals the name of the witness or the name of the suspect. In 1987 Donald Swanson's personal copy of Anderson's memoirs revealed that Swanson wrote that the suspect's name was Kosminski and that the witness was also a Jew. This above all has led those pro-Andersonians to wholeheartedly believe in Kosminski's guilt. Alternate Jewish suspects David Cohen and Nathan Kaminsky have also been suggested, resulting from the firm belief that Anderson oversaw a witness identification. Why Kosminski though?

Macnaghten's naming of Kosminski as suspect number two and Swanson's identification of Kosminski as Anderson's suspect has elevated him above Cohen and Kaminsky as a suspect. Obviously Macnaghten got the name Kosminski from Anderson. It has always been assumed that Swanson was at the witness identification, but why then would he need to reveal the name Kosminski to himself? There would be no reason to, implying that Swanson was not at the identification. More importantly, this implies that Swanson received the name Kosminski directly from Anderson. Kosminski as a suspect can be solely attributed to Anderson, and his feeding Macnaghten and Swanson that suspect's name has elevated Kosminski into primary suspect status.

The information about Kosminski that appears in Swanson's notes does not match with what we know about Aaron Kosminski. Some elements do fit Kosminski, while others are in direct contradiction, most notably that Kosminski did not die shortly after his transfer to Colney Hatch. Aaron Kosminski lived on for another 28 years. As such, the information provided to Swanson regarding Kosminski was not entirely correct. If Anderson were so sure that Kosminski was the murderer, wouldn't he have known that Kosminski was still alive while writing about him in 1910, 1907, 1901 and using Major Arthur Griffiths, under his pseudonym Alfred Aylmer, to declare that he had a perfectly plausible theory in 1895? Interestingly enough, it was in 1895 when *The Pall Mall Gazette* attributed the most respected theory to Swanson. For such an honorable, trustworthy and impeccable person as Robert Anderson, he just couldn't allow Swanson to receive any credit he felt he might have deserved.

This finally brings us back to the case of Dr. John Hewitt. Hewitt was a patient at Coton Hill Asylum during 1888. He was a voluntary patient, who could come and go as he pleased. After learning of Hicks' discovery, Wilson boldly stated that, if records showed Hewitt was not confined inside the asylum on the nights of the murders and had absented himself from Coton Hill of his own free will, then Hicks would finally have been the person who had positively identified the murderer. Before I reveal what the records showed regarding Hewitt, I will first explain the sole reason why Hewitt was suggested as Sickert's unnamed veterinary student in the first place.

In the 1947 and 1950 books by Sitwell, he does not mention that Sickert ever told him the name of the young veterinary student. In fact, the only tease to this man's identity was that Sickert said he had scribbled the name in a book he gave to his friend Albert Rutherston. This book is believed to have unfortunately been lost during the bombings of World War II. Again, it should be re-iterated that neither Sickert nor Sitwell ever provided a name to the young veterinary student suspect. So where did Hicks get the connection to the name Dr. John Hewitt from?

In 1970, theorist Donald McCormick released his second revised edition of his 1959 book *The Identity of Jack the Ripper*. McCormick revealed that the name of the young veterinary student was something like Druitt, Drewett, or Drewery. Interestingly enough, McCormick states he got this information from a doctor who knew Sickert and whose father had gone to school with Montague John Druitt. McCormick is wholly responsible for the naming, or approximate naming, of Sickert's suspect. There are specific reasons why.

McCormick's simple goal here is to eliminate Druitt from consideration as a suspect. At the release of McCormick's second revised edition in 1970, Druitt was considered the main suspect. By providing unsourced information about Druitt, McCormick attempted to further support his own suspect, Vassily Konovalov, by casting doubt on Druitt. McCormick even goes so far as to state that Walter Sickert was a suspect, which in 1970 he was not. He then concluded that Druitt could now be eliminated from consideration because of Sickert's tainted association to the case. It is an impressive move, yet an easy one, especially when McCormick creates all this source material out of thin air. One piece, however, was not created out of thin air, but stolen and used in McCormick's attempted ruse to abolish Druitt from the pool of suspects.

In 1959 researcher Dan Farson was gathering any and all information on "Jack the Ripper" for a television program. McCormick was on board as an adviser to the program. Within the documents sent to Farson was an Australian document allegedly written by a Lionel Druitt, Drewett, or Drewery who knew the murderer. This document was obviously seen by McCormick. This suspect was originally assumed to be Montague John Druitt, but further research by Keith Skinner and Martin Howells showed that the document pertained to another suspect, Frederick Bailey Deeming, who used the alias Drewen upon arriving in Australia. This information came to Farson prior to his receiving the Macnaghten memorandum that names the suspect Montague John Druitt. By the time Farson received the memorandum, the Australian document had vanished.

This is not a popularity contest, or, more to the point, a popularity contest in reverse.

In 1970 that Australian document would surface in the revised edition of *The Identity of Jack the Ripper*. Without mentioning anything about the actual document, McCormick stated that Sickert's young veterinary student's name was something like Druitt or Drewett. This wording is the link to the missing Australian document sent to Farson. More importantly, McCormick's misuse of stolen material for his own theory's benefit is the sole reason why Dr. John Hewitt was proposed by Hicks as the murderer.

The records from Coton Hill Asylum did reveal that Dr. Hewitt was confined inside the asylum on the nights of the murders. This information, made public in 1988, completely exonerated Hewitt as a suspect.

Remember what Wilson stated regarding the extraordinary find of researcher Hicks, that if one hundred year old records showed Hewitt was not confined during the nights of the murders then there would be no doubt that the case was solved. There would have been a suspect just like any other lesser or laughable suspect, with no hard evidence against him other than that there was no discernible proof that he were innocent, but who would have been viewed as a primary suspect. Basically Hewitt would have had no alibi for the murders, similar to Lewis Carroll and Joseph Fleming, but because of the intentional misuse of information by an untrustworthy researcher, the world would finally have a solution to the most historically unsolved murder case of all time, at least according to one of the foremost experts on the case.

Just imagine if the records were incomplete or showed that Hewitt was not in the asylum on those specific nights as well as most likely other random nights. Then we would have a real dilemma on our hands. We would now know that Hewitt should never have been suggested as a suspect in the first place, but there would be someone who had no alibi and the wholehearted endorsement of a leading expert. Luckily we do not have to face that problem.

Hewitt is meaningless as a suspect. In fact, he is a non-suspect as a result of academic research. The strange case of Dr. John Hewitt, and the circumstances surrounding his entire connection to these murders, however, should serve as an incredibly important parable about this case. Academic research will eventually discover additional instances similar in vital aspects to that of Hewitt and perhaps, just perhaps, we can start making a real dent in the suspect pool.

No evidence connects Druitt or Kosminski to the murders, yet their status as primary suspects will probably never change. No evidence connects Carroll or Fleming to the murders, and their status as laughable or non-suspects will also never change. Five men with similar stories, no hard evidence to link them to the murders and with the theories promoting their candidacy as suspects either erroneous, unconvincing or both. In what seems on the surface to be a monumental injustice, these five people, including Hewitt, are viewed in extremely different ways when it comes to discussing who is and who is not a viable suspect. It just does not seem fair to the suspects, who must remain as primary ones, that others can merely be laughed away simply because a researcher or theorist was not as convincing as they should have been.

If I had to personally rank these five suspects in the order from most likely to least likely, I would have to say Druitt, Kosminski, Fleming, Carroll, and exclude Hewitt, of course. I base this on nothing more than a gut feeling, so in actuality I have no real basis for listing these five suspects in this particular order. Any attempted ranking system within the parameters of this case would solely be based upon gut feelings and would differ with each individual researcher. Richard Wallace has a gut feeling. Mark King has a possible gut feeling. I can also positively state, without naming names, that currently two legendary researchers in this field have gut feelings that Montague John Druitt and Aaron Kosminski are the murderer. I personally have a gut feeling on who the murderer actually is. I'm sure you, the person reading this article, most likely have a gut feeling also. Colin Wilson had a gut feeling about Dr. John Hewitt, and still would if asylum records had mistakenly been lost or gone missing.

Sometimes the joy of solving this unsolvable case gets the better of all of us, and sometimes our frustrations are taken out against certain suspects, when they deserve their day in court, so to speak. Suspects, all of them, until they are cleared, deserve at least the appearance of equality, even if I don't believe they are on equal ground as viable suspects. Again it just is not fair to those who remain. This is not a popularity contest, or, more to the point, a popularity contest in reverse. It is an unsolved murder case, and as academics we should all remember this simple fact.

What does that really mean though? It means nothing in the long run. Or perhaps the next time a suspect is laughed at or viewed with the utmost approval as a viable candidate, a step back will be taken to embrace an overview of what this case really is. It is the unanswerable question. It is the ultimate in futility. It is... Well, you get the idea.

Who was "Jack the Ripper"? Hell if I know.

SOURCES:

Beadle, William, *Jack the Ripper: Anatomy of a Myth* (1995)

Begg, Paul, *Jack the Ripper: The Uncensored Facts* (1988)

Begg, Paul, Fido, Martin & Skinner, Keith, *The Jack the Ripper A - Z* (1996)

Campbell, Christy, *Fenian Fire: The British Government Plot to Assassinate Queen Victoria* (2004)

Evans, Stewart & Skinner, Keith, *The Ultimate Jack the Ripper Companion* (2000)

Jakubowski, Maxim & Braund, Nathan, *The Mammoth Book of Jack the Ripper* (1998)

McCormick, Donald, *The Identity of Jack the Ripper* (1970)

Ryder, Stephen P., *Casebook: Jack the Ripper*, www.casebook.org

Sitwell, Osbert, *A Free House* (1947)

Sitwell, Osbert, *Noble Essences* (1950)

Skinner, Keith & Howells, Martin, *The Ripper Legacy* (1987)

Wallace, Richard, *The Agony of Lewis Carroll* (1990)

Wallace, Richard, *Jack the Ripper: Light-Hearted Friend* (1996)

The Baltimore Ripper Conference in Review

This issue of *Ripper Notes* has two articles based upon presentations at the 2004 Ripper Conference in Baltimore April 16 through 18. So, what else happened there? Quite a bit.

Friday night, Michael Huie kicked off the weekend with his always well-received "Jack — a Solo Performance," which was followed by dinner, perusal of the wares in the book room, and socializing in the hotel bar.

Michael woke everyone up in the morning with "The Dead Raven Sketch" (ably assisted by Larry Barbee) and a dramatic reading of Poe's "The Raven." Bob Barnes followed with a presentation on Baltimore's most famous murders of the 19th century.

Stan Russo's turn at the podium came after lunch, when he dived into the various suspects of the case (see article). Harry Cook then discussed Jack London's book *People of the Abyss,* in which the American author tried living for a time in London's East End like the residents did. A slideshow with copious photos illustrated his points.

Leroy Stock, dressed as a Victorian auctioneer, took up the gavel and moved a variety of Ripper-related items to raise money for the 2006 conference

After a banquet dinner came the keynote presentation, "Veiling and Unveiling the Ripper Victims" by L. Perry Curtis. Using numerous slides, he compared early 20th century artwork with photos and illustrations related to the Whitechapel Murders

Sunday morning started with Chris George's look at the Jews of the East End and their various links to the Ripper case. John Hacker's presentation on technology in Ripperology (see article) came next, followed by an open mic session at which anyone could get up and discuss his or her favorite suspects.

And that ends an all too brief look at this year's conference. Brighton, England in 2005 is the next one scheduled. See www.ripperconference.com for updates.

Top: L. Perry Curtis gives his presentation.
Middle: Larry Barbee and Michael Huie pose with the raven prop.
Bottom: Conference attendees Emily Robinson and Kelly Robinson.
Conference photos copyright 2004 by Ally Reinecke and Stephen Ryder , used with permission

News & Notes

Forget about the Lusk kidney, we got a head!

Some of the attendees of this year's Ripper conference in Baltimore visited the American Dime Museum, which preserves the 19th century tradition of displaying an eccentric collection of natural and man-made curiosities like Fiji mermaids, shrunken heads and giant balls of twine. Candy Morgan has a web page with photos and descriptions of the trip they took.

One bit of news that stood out was that the Baltimore police allegedly found a head in the mail accompanied with a letter ending with a phrase reminiscent of the letter accompanying the piece of kidney George Lusk of the Whitechapel Vigilance Committee received.

Your inquisitive new *Ripper Notes* editor, a fan of the freak shows since he was a child, decided an quick investigation was in order, especially since it seemed to fit this issue's theme. American Dime Museum Director Dick Horne responded and provided the following details about the "Head of Harold":

"It is purported to be a head in a box which is accompanied by the following cryptic message (with numerous misspellings!); the remainder of the body is supposedly in Mississippi.

'Bewar - in this box be a head it belong to Harold he be foun with the rong gal an got stuck the rest is in Mississip I don no were but his head still laffin in this box. Catch me if you can'."

He thoughtfully adds that the head and story are "of questionable authenticity."

But wait, what about the mermaids?

Candy Morgan's page about the museum:
http://tinyurl.com/2ccsy

The museum's web site:
http://www.dimemuseum.net/

* * *

Casebook site gets editorial board

April must have been the month for announcing new editors, as the *Casebook: Jack the Ripper* web site got not one but two: Alex Chisolm and Chris Scott. Stephen P. Ryder, creator of the site, now becomes executive editor.

With the addition of two full-time editors to a site already bursting with content, Stephen promises that significant enhancements are on the way.

* * *

Abberline grave project started

Robin Lacey is heading up an effort to look into the possibility of getting a headstone placed on the grave of Frederick Abberline and his wife, Emma. Abberline was, of course, the police inspector most directly in charge of investigating the Whitechapel Murders.

Uncertain about whether the Abberlines wanted an unmarked grave or not, Robin is suggesting a discreet stone plaque instead of a larger gravestone. Currently all that exists is a small, deteriorating marker made of wood.

Robin would like to hear from those readers with thoughts on the matter or who would like to help out.

Email: robin.a.lacey@btinternet.com

Casebook **message board thread:**
http://casebook.org/forum/messages/4924/11186.html

* * *

A doubly disappointing Arthur Conan Doyle auction

An extensive collection of manuscripts and personal letters by the great Victorian mystery writer Arthur Conan Doyle sold at Christie's auction house for just under a million British pounds in May. Early expectations were that it would fetch at least twice that.

Sadly, the auction was preceded by the death in late March of Sherlock Homes expert Richard Lancelyn Green, who was found in his bed, surrounded by plush toy animals and a bottle of gin, with a shoelace tightened around his neck and held in place with a wooden spoon.

Friends said he had become highly emotional about the auction of the Conan Doyle papers, expressing the opinion that they should remain together and available for scholarly research. The court was told he had become obsessed and paranoid, claiming that "someone in America" was out to get him. Green also allegedly claimed that his house was bugged with covert listening devices.

The coroner was unable to rule whether this was a case of suicide, murder or an accidental death and, in late April, recorded an open verdict.

As Priscilla West, sister of the deceased, explained, and as quoted by the BBC, it all sounds like "the beginning of a thriller novel."

Robert F. Kennedy once claimed that the phrase "may you live in interesting times" is an ancient Chinese curse. With stories like this and the Whitechapel Murders, and with the Kennedy family too as far as that goes, dying in an interesting way might be a worse thing to wish upon someone.

* * *

From Hell to Kansas

It seems that the 1970s Wichita serial killer who named himself the BTK strangler in letters to police and news media is determined to be back in the limelight. First, he sent a letter in March of this year taking responsibility for a killing back in 1986, providing copies of photos he took of the victim and her driver's license. Since then he's sent two other messages, one to local police and one to television station KAKE. The latter contained a puzzle and photocopies of ID cards of two men, one a phone worker and another an employee of the school district. Police officials confirmed in late June that these are considered legitimate communications from the killer, presumably because they had the same identification marks set up in the '70s to verify the source.

The two big questions on the minds of residents and law enforcement officials are if the BTK strangler will kill again and where he was during the last decade and a half. Those people interested in the Great Victorian Mystery might look at this modern case and wonder what it might mean for deciding if any of the Ripper letters were authentic or if it would have been possible for Jack to have just stopped the killings on his own — or delayed them for so long that a continuation wouldn't have been linked to the originals.

* * *

Ripper leads new action figure set

If you've seen this issue's cover, you've already had a look at a portion of the new Jack the Ripper figure produced by McFarlane Toys and scheduled to be released in June.

The *McFarlane's Monsters 3 – Six Faces of Madness* set features a variety of historical characters who have earned mythic notoriety. Besides Jack, there's Countess Elizabeth Bathory (playing up the legends that she bathed in the blood of virgin girls to try to enhance her beauty), Vlad the Impaler (apparently about to skewer someone), the Russian mystic Rasputin (who is not only featured in the recent *Hellboy* movie but also has a bit part in the elaborate story Donald McCormick presented to try to support Pedachenko as a Ripper suspect), Attila the Hun (in a pose that would do Conan the Barbarian proud) and Billy the Kid (the Wild West gunfighter who seems just slightly out of his league compared to the others).

The characters will cost about $10 each. There's also an accessory pack available that has an assortment of add-ons to go with all six figures. Our boy Jack gets a nice Victorian lamp post and base.

The Ripper, as presented here, has a tool belt of nasty implements, a bag evidently containing some body part that is gushing blood like a fountain, and, oddly, what appears to be a prosthetic leg of some sort.

Some might object (and at least one person on the *Casebook* message boards has) to the level of gore and the artistic license in the figure, but then the line is marketed to adults and it's doubtful whether anyone would buy it thinking it's an accurate historical representation. They're not the sort of toys a mother would buy for a young child (although the Billy the Kid one might be unobjectionable), but, if you are into this sort of thing, the figures produced by Todd McFarlane are top of the line.

* * *

Of course, of course

The Associated Press reports that the perpetrator of a series of throat slashings in Tucson, Arizona, last summer has been caught. With a bit of an Andersonesque twist, it turns out that the culprit was secretly locked away -- and that his own kind, which knew all about the crimes, weren't

The McFarlane Monsters 3 line, featuring a version of Jack.

Figure images are copyright 2004 by McFarlane Toys and used with permission.

talking to the police about it.

Of course there was a good reason for that: The attacker and the victims in this case were horses.

Between July and September of 2003, police feared a maniac was cutting the throats of the animals at a ranch. The horses reportedly suffered wounds one to four inches long and one inch deep near their jugular veins, consistent with those inflicted by a knife. A large reward was offered, but no arrests were made.

Last fall, a ranch employee spotted one horse biting another. The offending animal was caged away from the rest, and then the attacks ended. It wasn't until June of this year, upon questioning by reporters, that the police confessed to knowing who was responsible. A spokesperson for the Pima County sheriff told the *Arizona Daily Star* that, although they don't have solid proof that the horse was responsible for all the attacks, they consider it likely and have closed the case.

Animal experts are already offering explanations for the unusual level of aggressiveness. Some are saying that past abuse was the likely root cause. Another expert was more blunt, saying, "Most likely this is just a mean horse."

Fans of radical Ripper theories take note: Wasn't it only after Louis Diemschutz left his pony alone with Elizabeth Stride and went to fetch a light that she was found to be cut and bleeding? And wasn't the site of Polly Nichols' murder right next to a horse stable? Hrmmmm...

* * *

Lizzie should have tried decaf

Not directly related to the Ripper but interesting in a "famous murder site becomes a tourist attraction" kind of way, the owners of the bed and breakfast at the Lizzie Borden house want to add a Starbucks coffee house to attract business.

New owners Donald Wood (there's the beginnings of a potential hatchet joke if I ever saw one) and Lee-Ann Wilbur (though that obvious Mr. Ed reference would have

worked better in the previous news brief) apparently haven't heard back from the corporation yet about whether there's a chance that they will be granted franchise rights. But, hey, even if the idea goes nowhere, at least they can say they took a whack at it.

* * *

Watch out for the uppercut

A New Jersey politician, while arguing that a decision that would allow Mike Tyson to box professionally in that state should be reversed, complained: "A convicted rapist, someone who assaulted a man by biting his ear. We might as well have Jack the Ripper come back and get a boxing license."

If they could pull it off, I bet that would do well on payperview TV. Too bad that Jack probably wouldn't come out of retirement for it though.

* * *

Another Ripper board game

Creator Tim Mandese and graphic designer Johnny Atomic have announced a new board game based upon the murders in the East End. Called RipperOpoly, it's obviously based upon the old standard Monopoly rules, but other than that not much is known. A picture on the product's web site (clearly an artist's rendition and not a photo of an actual game board) appears to show polished farthing pieces, barrels in place of houses, a deck of Ripper cards, and, fittingly, the utilities of the original game replaced by pubs.

Email requests by *Ripper Notes* for more information went unanswered. If we can get a hold of someone to respond to questions or maybe even get an opportunity to playtest the thing we will let you know about it in a future issue.

RipperOpoly web site:
> http://www.ripperopoly.com/

* * *

Does that make Sickert a feminist?

University of Gloucestershire professor Linden Peach told *The Citizen* in June that the same Walter Sickert paintings that novelist Patricia Cornwell claims are mutilated Ripper victims are actually based upon the works of feminist author Virginia Woolf.

Professor Peach (who probably gets asked all the time if he's seen Professor Plum in the library with the candlestick, poor guy — sorry, got board games on the brain) also claims that Woolf changed some of her writing based upon Sickert's influence.

* * *

See the paintings yourself

From July 9 through October 30, Abbot Hall Art Gallery will be hosting "The Human Canvas," an exhibition of 43 different Walter Sickert paintings. The included works were selected to span his career as an artist. Included are many of the pieces that the Ripper authors Stephen Knight, Jean Overton Fuller and, of course, Patricia Cornwell believe contain clues to the identity of the Whitechapel murderer, including "Ennui," "L'Affaire de Camden Town," "La Hollandaise," "Lazarus Breaks His Fast," and "Nuit d'Été."

On August 26, Rebecca Daniels will give a related lectured titled "Detection and Identity in Walter Sickert's Camden Town Series." Richard Shone will give a special walking tour of the exhibition on October 21. Lectures start at 6:30 p.m. and cost £7.50

Abbot Hall is located in Kendal, Cumbria, England. It is open Monday through Saturday from 10:30 am to 5 p.m. and is closed on Sundays. Regular admission is £4.75, which includes the Sickert exhibition.

A full-color exhibition catalogue featuring a new essay by Sickert biographer Matthew Sturgis is also being published. You can contact info@abbothall.org.uk for more information or to place an order for a copy when they come out.

Nuit d'Été
c. 1906, Oil on canvas.
Courtesy of Ivor Braka Ltd, London

La Hollandaise
c. 1906, Oil on canvas.
Tate. Purchased 1983

Abbot Hill Art Gallery web site:
http://www.abbothall.org.uk/

* * *

Ripper radio drama on the web

In June, Actors Unseen, a group that does radio theatre style dramas over the Internet, put on an original live show about the Ripper case called *Saucy Jack*. If you're interested in giving it a listen, see their web site for a current listing of rebroadcast dates.

Actors Unseen web site:
    http://www.actorssceneunseen.com/

* * *

Upcoming publications

Donald Rumbelow's updated *The Complete Jack the Ripper* (Penguin Books, ISBN 0140173951) is apparently available in the U.K. now, although the amazon.co.uk site lists the book as being produced in 1992, and the U.S. branch of the online bookstore seems to have not even heard of it. It looks like there's some sort of glitch in the listing. The only pricing information I can pull up is £8.99 for the one overseas.

Paul Begg's updated title, *Jack the Ripper: The Facts* (ISBN 1861056877), should be released by the end of July. It's list price here in the U.S. is $15.

Stewart P. Evans' new book: *Executioner: The Chronicles of James Berry, Victorian Hangman* (Sutton Publishing, ISBN 0750934077) has been released in the U.K. for £20 and should be making its way to the states for $27.95 soon. It is reviewed on page 89 of this issue.

Robert J. McLaughlin's book, *The First Jack the Ripper Victim Photographs* (Zwerghaus Books, ISBN 0973379405), is being planned as a limited press run of 200 copies later this summer. He is taking preorders through Judy Stock in the U.S. (email: needler@ntelos.net) or through Loretta Lay Books (see ad on the following page for available contact methods) or Murder One Books in the U.K. Robert says

the price will be in the neighborhood of £18, which should make it something like $27 U.S. using the "add 50 percent to the cost" rule of estimating such things.

The Jack the Ripper Suspects: Persons Cited by Investigators and Theorists (McFarland & Co., ISBN 0786417757) by Stan Russo may or may not be available by the time you read this. Amazon now shows an August 1 release date. It is expected to cost $45.

Stan tells *Ripper Notes* that he also has a suspect-based theory manuscript on the case already completed as well as a non-Ripper book called *The 50 Most Significant Individuals in Recorded History*. He is shopping both of those around to publishers.

Rumor has it that Richard Whittington-Egan's *The Quest for Jack the Ripper: A Literary History 1888-2000* is done all but for the bibliography. Of course this bibliography is alleged to be the largest ever assembled in a Ripper book, so who knows how long it will be before it actually comes out.

Martin Greenburg, well known for being an editor of literally hundreds of genre fiction anthologies, including the 1988 Ripper story collection *Red Jack,* is said to be churning out another one centered on the Whitechapel Fiend for an August release. The title for this one is listed as plain old *Jack the Ripper* (Ibooks, ISBN 0743493133). It's said to be a 336 page mass market paperback at a $6.99 price point.

In the too early to even think of a release date department, our very own Wolf Vanderlinden is looking at turning all the various research he did for the series of Carrie Brown articles into a full book.

Tom Slemen, the author of a number of books about the supernatural, is still talking about writing a book that names Claude Reignier Conder as the Ripper. The motive apparently is some revenge plot involving Satanic rituals against a gang of prostitutes (you get five guesses who they were) who stole from him. There's no word on how far along he might be or if he has any publisher lined up.

Here's one for off in the far flung future: Albert Borowitz, editor of the True Crime Series for the Kent State University Press, says that author Robin Odell is returning to Ripperology with a title tentatively called, well, *Ripperology*. Scheduled for a 2006 release, this would be his first Ripper project since a co-author spot on 1987's *Jack the Ripper: Summing Up and Verdict*. His first book in the field was way back in 1965 with the very hard to find and generally well-regarded for the time *Jack the Ripper in Fact and Fiction*.

If this new book comes out, the only thing that could beat it on the list of great comebacks would be if Jack really does come out of retirement to take up boxing in New Jersey...

Loretta Lay Books

Mail Order Only

24 Grampian Gardens.
London NW2 1JG
Tel 020 8455 3069
mobile 07947 573 326

www.laybooks.com

lorettalay@hotmail.com

Barker, **The Fatal Caress** h/b (ex. lib) £30
Barnard, **The Harlot Killer** p/b Presentation copy
    signed by author £50
Barry, **The Michaelmas Girls** hb/dw £40
Evans, **Executioner: The Chronicles of James
    Berry, Victorian Hangman** hb/dw £20
Evans/Skinner, **The Ultimate JtR Source Book**
    hb/dw Signed by both authors (labels) £30
Harris, **The Ripper File** hb/dw £30
Harrison, **The Diary of Jack the Ripper** hb/dw
    (1st US edn.) £10
Hodgson, **Jack the Ripper Through the Mists of
    Time** New p/b Signed £50
Leeson, **Lost London** h/b (red covers) £30
Miles, **One the Trail of a Dead Man: The Identity
    of JtR** New softcover Signed £16
Morrison, **Jimmy Kelly's Year of Ripper Murders**
    39pp. Booklet New £10
Odell, **Jack the Ripper in Fact and Fiction** p/b
    £30
Pulling **Mr. Punch and the Police** h/b £30
Sugden (Philip), **The Complete History of JtR**
    hb/dw £60
Turnbull (Peter), **The Killer Who Never Was**
    mint h/b £200
Tully, **The Secret of Prisoner 1167** p/b
    Signed label £9
Wilson/Odell, **JtR Summing Up and Verdict**
    hb/dw £30

The Bookcase

Executioner: The Chronicles of James Berry, Victorian Hangman

Stewart P. Evans

Type: Hardcover, Nonfiction
Length: 288 pages
Dimensions: 6.25" wide by 9.25" tall
Publisher: Sutton Publishing
Release date (US): August 2004
ISBN: 0750934077
List price: $27.95

Author Stewart Evans' latest book is a detailed look at the life of Victorian hangman James Berry. This is slightly afield of his usual Ripper-related tomes, but a number of characters and events do overlap. If you're looking to expand your knowledge while still focusing on some of the same familiar themes of the Autumn of Terror, you can't go wrong with this book.

The topic, which could have all too easily focused just on the lurid aspects if it were handled by an inferior author, gets a thorough scholarly treatment by a well-regarded historical researcher.

Berry apparently was a bit of a nonconformist even as a youth, as he got kicked out of school more than once for an advanced level of mischief. He also got into a bloody scuffle with a horse that tore his face open and, if his stories can be believed, saved the lives of not one but two people. Some of these youthful adventures sound reminiscent of something Mark Twain would tell about Tom Sawyer.

And already we run into what is probably the only weak part of the book. Berry loved to tell tales, and so much of this book is drawn from his own personal ver-sion of events that I was often not sure if what I was reading really was an accurate portrayal of how things happened. Evans often points out as the book progresses that Berry was no doubt trying to cast himself in a favorable light, but at a certain level it probably wasn't enough of a warning. I know that when other people's accounts make their way into the narrative, they are often jarring in just how different they are from everything else we've been told.

And sometimes the problem is knowing which James Berry to trust. Which should hold more weight, the memoirs of the man defending his career and supporting the necessity of the death penalty or the ser-mons of an evangelist later in life condemn-ing hanging as immoral? Or perhaps the later letter from the same man begging to get his old job back?

Obviously Berry was very conflicted about his line of work, so contradictory statements are to be expected. It also is fairly apparent that the controversy over the death penalty as well as personal differences biased some of the accounts of other people. It all left me wishing that there were some solid and reliable reports from a neutral third party. Evans certainly can't be faulted for not using sources he didn't or couldn't have, but I would have appreciated a bit more of the author's perspective to try to sort it all out. Of course that's a personal preference, and I'm sure others would have complained if he editorialized more

The meat of the book is an account of the crimes of the various characters Berry would eventually end up executing. As such, it is a nice overview of a wide variety of Victorian murder cases. A number of them have links in one way or another to the notorious Jack the Ripper crimes.

Most notably there is William Henry Bury, who seems to have been the person Berry believed was responsible for the notorious Whitechapel murders of 1888. Of course, as happens all too frequently in this field, the theorizing appears to have a few disturbing leaps of logic as well as mere anecdotes used as evidence. For example, Berry — or a ghostwriter — made much out of the alleged similarity between Bury's handwriting and that of a writer of a letter claiming to be from the killer, except that the letter in question was sent well after Bury had already been executed. Similarly, Berry alleges that policemen showed up at the execution and wanted to try to get the hangman to make the condemned man confess to the Ripper murders. Beyond the fact that Berry has shown himself to be a chronic teller of tales of dubious authenticity, even if it were true it'd just mean that some officials thought there might be a link, which isn't necessarily all that compelling as far as evidence goes.

There is also Mary Wheeler, better known to history as Mary Eleanor Pearcey, who killed her lover's wife and child out of jealously and disposed of the bodies with a baby buggy. At least one author has credited her with the murders in the Autumn of Terror as a kind of Jill the Ripper. While that particular theory seems pretty drastically lacking, we do get some interesting information about the case. Most surprising for me was that Berry called her the most beautiful criminal he ever had to hang. Based upon the image of her passed down to us through a hideous gap-toothed wax figure that looks like a cross between Alfalfa of *The Little Rascals* and Alfred E. Neuman of *Mad* magazine fame, I would have thought that even half the men he hanged could be called prettier. Evans points out, however, that she was actually quite well known at the time for her beauty, having seduced many a man in her day.

Of course we can't forget Israel Lipski, the Jewish man convicted of poisoning a woman in the East End. He was responsible for turning "Lipski" into a racially-charged epithet. We recognize the term these days because it got shouted at a witness who saw Elizabeth Stride being attacked on the night she was killed. Reading about the threat of racial violence on the day of the execution underscores the potential for rioting a year later based upon the apparent Jewish reference in the Goulston Street Grafitto and the well-publicized search for the Jewish suspect Leather Apron during the killings that later became famous as the Ripper murders.

The book also introduces a number of other interesting personalities who found themselves with ropes around their necks. There's Dr. Phillip Henry Cross, who offed his wife so he could marry a nanny about a third his age; John Lee, who earned himself a pardon the hard way after several pulls of the lever still didn't send him dropping to his death; Elizabeth Berry, who not only shared the hangman's last name but actually went out on a date with him when they were both younger; and many more.

The parts I found most fascinating were the men from the upper classes who paid their way on as assistants to the executioner and the ever present threat of danger whenever Berry had job to do in Ireland. When people plunging to their dooms looks like it might get slightly tiresome, you can always count on the Irish to liven things up.

Those people who think that there must be some sort of significance in the fact that Catherine Eddowes called herself Mary Ann Kelly on the night she was killed while the next Ripper victim was named Mary Jane Kelly might want to take note that Berry's mother's maiden name was Mary Ann Kelley. Of course that's just a coincidence, but I'm sure there is a twisted Ripper theory waiting to be dreamed up out of that bit of information, should anyone want to stoop that low.

While not quite as lavishly illustrated as the author's other work — like the extensive number of photos in *The Ultimate Jack the Ripper Companion* or the color interior of *Jack the Ripper: Letters from Hell* — this book does have a decent collection of images in the center, though nothing spectacular.

Those looking to try to judge the Great Victorian Mystery in context should read *Executioner* for points of comparison to other crimes. It's also good to have just for extra general knowledge of the Victorian era. I recommend it to *Ripper Notes* readers.

* * *

Some Danger Involved

Will Thomas

Type: Hardcover, Fiction
Length: 288 pages
Dimensions: 5.75" wide by 8.66" tall
Publisher: Touchstone Books
Release date: June 2004
ISBN: 0743256182
List price: $22.95

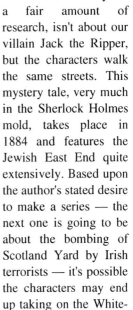

This debut novel by Will Thomas, a librarian living in Oklahoma who clearly did a fair amount of research, isn't about our villain Jack the Ripper, but the characters walk the same streets. This mystery tale, very much in the Sherlock Holmes mold, takes place in 1884 and features the Jewish East End quite extensively. Based upon the author's stated desire to make a series — the next one is going to be about the bombing of Scotland Yard by Irish terrorists — it's possible the characters may end up taking on the Whitechapel Fiend in future installments.

And what characters they are. Thomas really knows how to give us protagonists we can cheer for.

We start out with Thomas Llewelyn, a man with an Oxford education. Two of them, in fact, if you count the prison as well as the university. He is planning to pull a Druitt into the Thames River if he can't find a way to support himself soon. He applies for a job that, as the newspaper ad and the book's title both warn, might be a bit difficult now and then. In fact, the death of the previous individual who held it is what prompted the opening. Llewelyn then proceeds to experience a very unorthodox interview, one which I won't spoil any of the pleasure of reading by revealing details here.

Enquiry agent Cyrus Barker is the one looking for a man of very specific talents to assist him, and he decides that Llewelyn is the one for the job. Barker is a cliché — a brilliant but eccentric Victorian private investigator. But then the idea is used in a lot of stories because it works so well for dramatic purposes. If anything, *Some Danger Involved* exploits it even better than most.

Llewelyn finds himself suddenly with a new job, new clothes, and a new place to live — one with a French chef, no less. Part of the joy of reading the book is watching the novice assistant adapt to his situation.

Soon they are called to a case, and it's a rather troublesome one A young Jewish student named Louis Pokrzya has been crucified, and the Jewish board of deputies wants Barker to help bring the guilty party to justice. They fear an increase of anti-Semitic violence and want to try to get things under control before they get any worse. So Barker and Llewelyn explore the areas where various ethnic populations live and try to find the root of the mystery.

The only real downfall to the book is the rather anticlimactic ending. In fact, some mystery fans may feel cheated. If you are looking for a period piece that explores Victorian London's underbelly and has a great set of well imagined and complex personalities, this book should be on your to read list. Those more interested in trying to solve the whodunnit aspects before the main

character may want to give it a pass, as that's not exactly the strength of the book. In either case, it is a strong debut for an author writing about a period near and dear to the hearts of most Ripper fans.

* * *

Ripperologist #53

As a new editor here, I wasn't sure I should review other Jack the Ripper magazines. But then the others have comments about each other, so who am I to break the trend?

The only periodical I have received since putting on the editor's cap is the May 2004 *Ripperologist*. The cover is an illustration for Jan Bondeson's article about DNA testing. The photo features Anna Anderson, who had many people convinced that she was Anastasia Romanov until mitochondrial DNA comparisons ruled that out. The photo and the cover in general are very green, perhaps from an *Incredible Hulk* influence on the design.

Inside, Executive Editor Paul Begg starts us off with an editorial about how assumptions can be bad. I think most everyone would agree with that. Of course I don't think that stops anyone from doing it just the same.

Bondeson's article comes next, which has fascinating information about what DNA testing had to say about the claims of different people to being lost royalty of various countries. Patricia Cornwell's tests to try to link Sickert to letters claiming to be from the Ripper are discussed briefly and dismissed as a "blatant misuse" of technology. I'm sure supporters of her theory would need a more thorough explanation before they would agree, but then that probably goes without saying no matter how long the topic would have been discussed.

Scott Nelson's piece is a nice discussion of the Polish Jew theory that is based upon the statements of some police officials years after the case, but with some twists of his own. For one, he suggests that the Seaside Home witness (the alleged identification of a mental patient as the Ripper) was Joseph Levy and not Joseph Lawende, as is often believed. Although Levy had testified at Catherine Eddowes' inquest that he couldn't identify the person seen with her outside of Mitre Square, Nelson finds some wiggle room around that statement. There is a lot of research into various family relations, and a plausible scenario is presented, albeit one with a number of assumptions that might not hold up.

Christopher T. George has a good roundup of Jewish links to the East End and the Ripper case, presumably largely based upon his presentation at the 2004 Ripper Conference in Baltimore. Later in the issue he reviews the conference and presents an interview with yours truly about my plans for *Ripper Notes*, which if you're reading this you've already largely seen the results of. (Oh, and in case you were wondering, the thing that I'm holding in the photo is a nearly life-sized human head made of glass. It's either clever or silly, your pick.)

Ripperologist spends a lot of time at rounding up little snippets of information more or less related to the case. This issue has extensive newspaper clips, news briefs, reviews, and so forth totaling about a third of the issue's 53 pages.

Other than that, we have Rob Hills advocating what could be an interesting new theory about cat meat man James Haldiman as a Ripper suspect if it were developed a lot more, Christopher-Michael DiGrazia asking whether fiction can help enlighten views on the case, Coral Kelly discussing the Peabody buildings, and Eduardo Zinno giving Sir Peter Ustinov a full page obituary (apparently that's because Ustinov hosted a TV special about Jack the Ripper once).

Overall, the content is highly variable, but when it's good there's no denying it. Everyone's tastes differ, though, so no doubt the parts I found weakest were just as loved by someone else reading it.

Are you an author or publisher with a book (or other product) you'd like to see reviewed in this magazine? *Ripper Notes* welcomes review copies. They can be mailed to:

Dan Norder, editor
Ripper Notes
2 N. Lincoln Ridge Dr. #521
Madison, WI 53719

If your book isn't ready for a review yet but you'd like to be mentioned in the "News & Notes" section, drop us a line at the above address, or email the editor at dan@norder.com with your information.

Coming in October's "Madmen, Myths & Magic" issue of *Ripper Notes*...

Jan Bondeson gives a history of serial sadistic stabbers

Editor **Dan Norder** examines some of the legends that got linked to the case

Thomas Wescott talks "Jack the Ripper, Jesus Christ & the Lindbergh Kidnapping"

Bernard Brown's "The Witches of Whitechapel"

Plus other articles and regular features...

The Inquest

Welcome to "The Inquest." I'm Jennifer Pegg and I write this new column. I am a 20 year old undergraduate student from the UK. I have been interested in Ripperology for just over four years since discovering the debates about the identity of the killer in the books on display in the local library. I still haven't made up my mind on a suspect! You may know me as a regular on *Casebook: Jack the Ripper.* My other interests include the life and times of Victorian spiritualist Robert James Lees.

This May I conducted a short sample survey so that we could bring you a flavour of how this column will work in future issues. The sample was conducted with the help of the readers of the *Casebook,* **JTRForums.com** and the Yahoo! Ripper Group. I would like to thank all you who took the time to respond so I would have something to write about in this issue.

Here are some of the comments of those who took part: -

Survey responses are enclosed within quotation marks, Edits for clarity sake are in brackets. Parenthetical statements and emphasized words were retained as they were in the original answers. Some replies were truncated for space. — the Editor

Question 1: How important do you think the Jack the Ripper letters are for the purpose of solving the case?

"I don't think the Ripper letters can tell us anything useful. Most people agree Jack the Ripper probably didn't write them anyway."

"Of the numerous Jack The Ripper letters written I believe that a few may be of purpose."

"The 'From Hell' letter might prove useful. I doubt the authenticity of all the other letters I've seen. I doubt 'From Hell' as well, but the kidney and lack of a signature make me think it might be real Ripper correspondence."

"I do not think the letters are particularly important, with the possible exception of the Lusk letter. But as the kidney is missing, that too must remain dubious."

"The letters are of no use in solving the case, save that we all owe a debt of gratitude to the person whose letter coined the term Jack the Ripper. Without that catchy name the Whitechapel murders would have remained as little remembered as the contemporaneous 'torso murders.' As the 20th century taught us, it is all in the advertising, and Jack the Ripper was as inspired as the 'Marlboro Man.'"

"The letters, especially those that we are most aware of, are nothing more than a colorful distraction, albeit one that has served very effectively to perpetuate myths and feed already bloated cash cows. The authorities at the time, after initial consideration, apparently thought they were of little use; Modern assessments have not done much to restore any importance and I concur with those who would dismiss these missives as merely social and historical curiosities."

"Wow, that's a toughie. While I think the letters are too often disregarded out of hand, since none contain text that **only** could have come from the killer, none could therefore be used as a 'smoking gun' against a suspect, even if it were proven who [wrote them.] I don't see the letters as being crucial to solving the case, but could certainly add enlightenment on a particular suspect should it be proven he wrote [one or more]."

"Somewhat important (handwriting analysis of known suspects) — but many might be pranks."

"They are of no importance at all."

It appears that most of those who took part in the survey did not think that the

letters were of much or any importance. None of you replied that they were either important or very important. I guess this will come as somewhat of a blow to Patricia Cornwell whose answer would probably have been that they are very important, as she uses them as part of the case against the suspect Walter Sickert. However, it appears the Lusk/From Hell letter may be favoured as a better prospect than the rest for the purposes of solving the case.

Question 2: Which non-fiction book based on the case of Jack The Ripper do you believe to be the best?

Though we only asked for one book some people felt that more than one was worthy of a mention. Here are some of the reasons given for the choices made: -

"The *Complete History of Jack the Ripper* by Sugden, but I very pointedly [warn] against reading too much into the chapter on Chapman. Beyond that, though, I feel the book gives a good, fairly up-to-date overview of the crimes, the investigation and the various theories."

The same contributor also recommended the "*A-Z* [Fido, Begg and Skinner]

and *The Ultimate Jack the Ripper Companion* [Evans and Skinner]. The former because while growing increasingly out of date it remains the handiest reference for the basic facts and the latter because easy access to documents and statements is essential to properly study of the case.'"

"Ivor Edwards' *Jack The Ripper's Black Magic Rituals* is my favorite as far as one with a **suspect** basis. Phil Sugden's *Complete History Of Jack The Ripper* would be my favorite **detail** based book."

"At this very moment, I have to call it a draw between Philip Sugden's *The Life and Times of Jack the Ripper* and *The Pocket Essential Jack the Ripper* by Mark Whitehead and Miriam Rivett. I think these two are the most concise, up to date and (more importantly) unbiased accounts of the murders."

"Of the only seven or eight I've read: P. Cornwell's *Portrait...* and the *Diary* caught my interest most. Cornwell, because her book built a pretty believable case; the *Diary* for similar reasons. I'm currently reading M. Harris' *True Face of Jack the Ripper;* and midway through, I'm already having a hard time believing the case as it is predicated on the statements of an apparent loon (the woman into black magic, who 'knew' the Ripper)."

"*The Ultimate Jack The Ripper Companion* [by] Evans and Skinner. I have found it to be an invaluable resource aid."

"I would have to say *The Ultimate Sourcebook* because it is so comprehensive and neutral."

"*The Ultimate Jack the Ripper Companion*, because it contains the actual files, is unbiased, and is from the trustworthy hand of Stewart Evans (along with Keith Skinner)."

"Bedrock fact must take priority. I have read some great JTR books, but I guess the Evans and Skinner *Ultimate Jack The Ripper Sourcebook* is essential."

It is worth reminding readers that *The Ultimate Jack The Ripper Companion* and *Sourcebook* are in fact the same book under different titles. Amongst those who took part in the sample survey it is the undoubted favourite. Also praised highly (especially considering this was only a small scale sample survey) was Philip Sugden's *The Complete History Of Jack The Ripper.*

Question 3: How reliable or useful do you consider eyewitness testimony to be for the purpose of identifying Jack the Ripper?

"I believe that all the eyewitness testimony should be viewed individually."

"Eyewitness testimony may be important to the Polish Jew theory, and to the Hutchinson theory (in the latter case, because of what it might tell us about the witness himself). But in general I think the eyewitness testimony should be treated with a great deal of caution."

"Little to none. The statements vary so much, are tinged with prejudice, and smack of someone wanting fame and attention at times. I also think it likely the Ripper may very well have made use of some sort of disguise."

"There's such a pile of witness identifications that a) don't mesh with one another, b) can't be conclusively proven to

have been the murderer of the victim they were spotted with, or c) are so vague in their details they could've been anybody, that I don't see how any known witness description could alone 'identify' the Ripper, though, they certainly can and do bolster a case for a suspect, or help to provide additional information on a particular suspect."

"Reliability = 50%. Usefulness = 60%"

"Nothing that we have heard from the eyewitness testimonies can be used to specifically finger any of the popular 'suspects.' Vaguely circumstantial 'evidence' may be applied to too many suspects; I think that the testimonies of (for example) Schwartz or Lawende would have benefited the police at the time immeasurably more than it would us today; The statements survive, but the impressions they made upon those who were in the best positions professionally to determine their importance have become obscure, rendering the words somewhat hollow and frustratingly inconclusive."

"I consider the various eyewitness accounts to be of some utility. Such accounts are always of dubious worth in regard to particulars and most of the Ripper 'sightings' were also made from a distance and under less than optimal lighting conditions. Still, if the descriptions are run through a relatively coarse filter certain patterns emerge: an individual of no more than middling height for the era, dressed conventionally for area and, while age is very difficult to determine from a glance or two, surely not someone very young or very old. For the most part, the various witness descriptions do perform a negative function by pretty well eliminating some of the more outré suspects like Tumblety because of his height and penchant for exotic dress.'

"Not particularly reliable but still possibly useful. I doubt Hutchinson's story, but the first man Schwartz spotted may have been Stride's killer."

"Close to zero."

Not many of the respondents seemed to think that the eyewitness accounts could be of much use, though some felt they could be of more helpful than others.

Question 4: Do you think Jack the Ripper necessarily had any medical knowledge or ability?

There was one straight to the point "No." Other answers:-

"I do not believe he was necessarily a doctor. However some degree of knowledge may have been required in order to find organs presuming Jack knew what he was looking for and didn't just take what he could find."

"I don't believe that Jack the Ripper had any medical knowledge other than a basic understanding of the human body."

"Absolutely nothing that resembles a surgical procedure is to be found in any of the murders. If the perpetrator was consciously seeking specific organs, I think you would have seen a bit more precision and a bit less of tossing entrails about. Arguing haste would be a tough sell in the case of Catherine Eddowes, considering the delicate work that was done on her face. Knowing how to use a sharp knife is not confined to the medical professions. I'd bet the average Ripperologist has learned enough about throat-cutting and the location of certain organs to rival the 'knowledge' and 'ability' of the Whitechapel murderer."

"I think JTR had some medical knowledge (i.e. the location of the kidney)."

"I think he knew some anatomy, but he did not necessarily have any actual medical knowledge training, or ability."

"Deserves more attention that it has received [...] That does not mean Jack was a doctor or ever trained as a doctor, but he had learned something about human anatomy by observation or from books. The uterus is normally a small organ amidst a lot of human plumbing and to quickly find and remove it [...] calls for a fair degree of know-how about the human anatomy. [...] Cutting a throat is a learned technique. Give someone a knife and they will instinctually stab or slash, but to cleanly sever the carotid in one or two passes — that was learned somewhere."

"A man self-taught by reading (ana-tomy books, here) can do many things almost equally to school-taught men; but as to whether any real 'doctor-type' skills were exhibited by the killer - I do not feel so. He knew where to cut (it's hard not to know where a woman's sex organs are); knew the locations of kidneys, etc. — but what real skills are necessary to butcher a person?"

"Yes, though I don't believe he was an active doctor/surgeon. The medical opinion of the time weighed heavily in favour of the Ripper having had some medical knowledge, and I don't understand why so many investigators today overlook this or disregard this opinion."

"Yes. D'onston had been a surgeon at the age of 19 in Italy."

The general view seems to be that some sort of knowledge was needed but that the killer was not necessarily a doctor in the qualified sense .

Question 5: Did Jack the Ripper write the Goulston Street Graffito?

Two contributors answered with a simple "yes," and one with a "In short, no." Other responses included:-

"No, I don't think Jack wrote the graffito… mainly because the provenance of the apron part from Mitre Square to Goulston Street is so tenuous as to make any comments about the graffito a waste of time. And especially since the 'message' is so ambiguous. I'm not sure, even if we had an iron-clad guarantee it was the Ripper's work, what would gained besides knowing the Ripper wrote in a 'schoolboy's round hand.' "

"I doubt if Jack wrote the graffito. Why would he run the risk of writing this message? Why not pin a pre-written message to the body? If he was trying to communicate, why write such a vague message, and in such small lettering?"

"I do not believe that he did. Either his dropping the apron there was just another of the monstrous coincidences of the case, or he did so deliberately to take advantage of an existing graffito that he saw. I personally favour the coincidence scenario."

"Uncertain. And even if he did, its meaning is unclear, and too great an importance has been placed on it as far as I'm concerned: little handwriting analysis would be gained (there is a vast difference in how one writes a letter, than how one writes on a wall); it shows the Ripper's path (if he wrote it); only the scrap of bloody cloth left at the scene holds any real value."

"It is possible that Jack the Ripper wrote the Goulston Street graffito, as part of the victims bloodied apron was found under it."

"I believe that it was most probably written by the person who murdered Catherine Eddowes... If the police could have found someone who could acknowledge the previous existence of the writing, it would have been unnecessary for Sir Charles Warren to publicly issue a statement regarding the word 'juwes.' It seems that distancing the graffito from the crime would have been a much easier course, had it been an option. And if the murderer had taken the time to nick the eyelids, etc., of Eddowes, I doubt that it would have seemed to him any more precarious to chalk a short message, regardless of its intended meaning."

Those who responded clearly did not agree on whether Jack wrote the graffito. Many of you questioned why Jack would have spent time and risk being caught in order to write such a message. Whilst for others the presence of the apron was something that helped to determine the validity of the writing.

* * *

The first full survey is below. The questions for the October issue of "The Inquest" are meant to be general introductory questions. Answers are completely confidential, and we will not use your name in our analysis unless you expressly give permission to. Please give as long or as short of an answer as you wish. Feel free to skip any question by writing no comment.

"The Inquest" Ripper survey questions for the October 2004 issue:

Question 1:
Who do you feel is the most likely suspect to have been Jack the Ripper? Or, if not a suspect, what do you consider the most likely theory to explain the murders?

Question 2:
Which suspect or theory do you think is the least likely to be true?

Question 3:
Do you believe the police did all they could to catch the killer? If the killings had taken place today could the police have caught the killer?

Question 4:
What impact do you think theories suggested by high profile people and popular books and films have on the general public? Do you think they are helpful in solving the case?

Question 5:
What do you see as the greatest challenge to Ripperology in the near future?

Question 6:
Which Ripperologist do you admire the most?

Question 7:
If you could offer one piece of advice to someone starting out investigating the case of Jack the Ripper, what would it be?

Survey answers can be emailed to the address **rippersurvey@yahoo.co.uk** or sent through the *Ripper Notes* website at: **www.RipperNotes.com/inquest.html**

If you'd rather send your responses via regular postal mail, they can be addressed to the *Ripper Notes* editor (see p. 1 for the address). Please respond by August 31. We look forward to hearing your views on these topics.

Lusk Kidney Revelation:
A London Hospital Surgeon Speaks

By Thomas C. Wescott

*Thomas C.Wescott is a long time contributor and supporter of **Ripper Notes**. Some of his previous articles include "Sickert, Ennui and the Ripper Letters" and "An Inspiration 'From Hell'?" He can be reached by email at* tcwes@aol.com *and welcomes comments about this article.*

When PC William Pennett of H-Division was making his rounds on the morning of September 10th, 1889, he made a discovery that would, for a short time, raise the spectre of Jack the Ripper. In his own words, PC Pennett sets the scene:

"I was passing along Pinchin-street, at the foot of Backchurch-lane, about a quarter-past five this morning, when I saw lying on the ground the trunk of a woman, the head and legs of which had been severed and were not present. The body was quite naked, except for a piece of torn linen which might have been a shift or portion of a pair of drawers, thrown over it. The body was fearfully disemboweled, and was marked as if it had been carried in a sack. My own opinion is that it had been so conveyed to the spot where I found it. The stench was something terrific. It would have been impossible to have passed it."

Pall Mall Gazette, Sept.10, 1889

Although the idea might seem preposterous to us now, there was a very strong opinion at the time that the whole affair of the "Pinchin Street torso," as it has since become known, had been a hoax, perpetrated by medical students from the London Hospital. These same medical students —

apparently held in somewhat low regard by the denizens of East London — had, just the year before, been the object of much finger-pointing when chairman of the Whitechapel Vigilance Committee, George Lusk, opened a small parcel to find a portion of a human kidney, purportedly taken from the body of Catherine Eddowes by none other than Jack the Ripper.

The logic was sound; if the kidney had not come from Eddowes, which quite possibly was the case, then suspicion would naturally fall on those working or residing in the one place in the East End where human organs could easily be procured — the London Hospital. And as a doctor, or more specifically an English doctor, was seen as being above such gruesome shenanigans, a young medical student would be the logical suspect. Even today this theory is accepted by those who believe George Lusk to have been the victim of a senseless prank. Unfortunately, we know very little about how a dissecting room operated in late 19th Century London, or how easy or difficult it would have been to obtain such an item as a human kidney, to say nothing of an entire torso, without raising any eyebrows. But the following interview with an unnamed London Hospital surgeon, first appearing in the *Pall Mall Gazette* and lost and forgotten until its appearance here, gives us a small peek behind the closed doors of a Victorian dissecting room:

Interview with a London Hospital Surgeon
What He Thinks of the Medical Hoax Theory

Wishing to find out whether there is anything in the theory which has been suggested, and which has become somewhat popular in the East-end, that the trunk of the woman found in Pinchin-street last Tuesday morning has come from some dissecting room, a correspondent of the Pall Mall Gazette called at the London Hospital and had a chat with one of the resident surgeons.

"I am not at all surprised," said the doctor, smiling, "that many people think this affair a hoax on the part of medical students. It is, of course, within the range of possibility that students may get possession of a body; but as to the theory that this particular trunk has been taken from some dissecting room, it is really, in my opinion, absurd. It is the most unlikely thing in the world that a trunk should be in the state in which I understand this one to be in, after being in the dissecting-room. It is against dissecting-room rules that it should be as it is."

"Will you kindly explain how?"

"Well, you see there are standing rules for dissecting bodies. The corpse is dissected in a thoroughly systematic fashion. It is left almost entirely to the students. The body is laid out on the dissecting table and each student takes a certain part. By the time a body is dissected it is, as you may imagine, quite unrecognizable."

"Is it a fact, as you have seen alleged, that it is a common thing for students to possess themselves of portions of bodies after dissection?"

"Oh, yes. They often take away a foot or a hand, but it is not very likely that they would cart home a head or a leg."

"What, may I ask, is done with the remains after dissection?"

"The different portions are collected and the whole buried together."

"May I inquire where you get your dissecting room subjects from here?"

"We get them generally from the workhouse."

"Could students obtain a body from the workhouse on their own account?"

"Well, that I can't say. It might be possible for them to do so. I may observe so long as I remember that even if this trunk affair is a hoax by medical students, none of our young men have anything to do with it, because they are all away just now. This is vacation time, and the dissecting-room is not open."

"From what you have heard about this trunk, do you think that great surgical skill must have been possessed by the person or persons who disemboweled it?"

"Of course I have not seen the remains, and I can only go by what I have read and heard; but let me say that it is ridiculous to talk about surgical skill in the way that people are doing with the Whitechapel horrors. Any butcher could do what has been done in any of the cases, this trunk case included. One does not necessarily require to be a doctor or a medical student to be able to dismember a body. I think there has been rather too much made of this point in connection with the murders."

Pall Mall Gazette, Sept.13, 1889

This interview is remarkable not only in the light it sheds on the likelihood of the medical hoax theory, but in how nonchalant the good doctor is in defending his students, hospital, and profession; he seems to have had no problem sharing with the readers that

This detail from a 1751 engraving by William Hogarth titled "The Reward of Cruelty" (plate IV of "The Four Stages of Cruelty") depicts the fears that the British public had about what happened to corpses in the Surgeon's Hall.

If the surgeon quoted in the Sept. 13, 1889, *Pall Mall Gazette* article is any indication, those fears may have been warranted even as late as the end of the 19th Century.

it's a matter of course for students to abscond with the foot or hand of their loved ones, while reassuring the public that "it is not very likely that they would cart home a head or a leg"!

Although it doesn't seem likely that the Pinchin Street torso was the work of medical students, the information provided here clearly indicates that the process of dissection was not strictly supervised, if supervised at all, and that anyone in the hospital with a mind to obtaining a body part, such as a human kidney, could have done so without risk of capture or punishment, should they have been a doctor, a medical student, a porter... or, just perhaps, a patient.

Case Insensitive: A Philadelphia Ripping

By Howard Brown

Howard Brown lives in Philadelphia. This is his first article for **Ripper Notes**.

February 28th, 2003, was almost like any other Winter day in Philadelphia. Cold, raw, and typically overcast. Being that it was a Friday, the only bright spot was that the weekend was approaching. In North Philadelphia, for many, that meant a rejuvenation of drug sales on the meanest streets of the city. This, after all, is the area many call the Badlands. But for one man, Willie "Pete" Kent, this day went from bad to worse in a way that would echo the far more famous crimes of Jack the Ripper more than a century before.

The Badlands of Philadelphia are the area that branch out from Broad Street, from Erie Avenue in the north to Spring Garden in the south, Ridge Avenue on the west to Front St. on the east side. Almost exclusively an Afro-American and Hispanic enclave, the Badlands are Philadelphia's Whitechapel and in more ways than one, as we shall see.

A testament to White flight and the relocation of plants, mills, and once thriving factories to the suburbs and Sun Belt, the Badlands are an area where, at night, anything goes. Police presence can usually be found in force on the main drag, Broad Street, patrolling and ostensibly stifling potential acts of prostitution. However, it's the side streets where, from row homes and dark alleys, that much of the nocturnal activity occurs. Vacant lots and abandoned buildings are the norm, not the exception. Boarded-up homes and homes barricaded from within by drug dealers are quite common.

Paul Begg's book *Jack the Ripper: The Definitive History* has a terrific history of how the slums in the East End of London came about. The East End of the late 19th Century was once a thriving community with 50,000 people employed in the silk industry alone in 1854. Just 25 years later that figure had shrunk to 3,000.

So too, North Philadelphia had once thrived. Those were the old days, however. Dozens of large employers moved away, leaving a huge portion of Philadelphia's working class blacks scrambling for whatever jobs were available.

It is the old days of 1950s Philadelphia that attracted Willie "Pete" Kent to the city in the first place. Born on May 11th, 1942, in Savannah, Georgia, Willie James Kent was adopted into a family of 15 children. His mother had nicknamed him "Pete Chachi" for reasons unknown, but the "Pete" part remained with him. Kent, a man barely 5 feet tall, became a union steel and iron cutter, as well as a deacon at a nearby church. He met a woman, Earthadine Christy, with whom he had one daughter, but they never married. Willie Kent and his lady friend were neighborhood fixtures in North Philadelphia. Kent was active in political causes

Letrese Bryant, his now grown daughter, said that Kent would stay at her home at times, but that he inevitably would go out to live on the streets. He had been doing so for six years. David's Food Market, the corner grocery where Kent helped out for the two decades before his death, is about 25 blocks away from her home. His bosses thought the world of him and considered him a part of their family. Kent lived on a monthly disability check and the money he made at the market.

Willie "Pete" Kent definitely deserved better than the way they found him on that cold, gray day in February, 2003. Dumped in an alley on 1520 Eighth Street in the

Badlands, Pete was found with a rope around his neck, frozen and most definitely dead.

Along with the apparent garroting, Kent was "laid open like a frog in biology class," according to one investigator. His throat was slashed and — in a twist that calls to mind the Fiend of Whitechapel — his heart, liver and kidney were missing. Police Commissioner Sylvester Johnson was heard to say on television, "Whoever did this knew what they were doing."

The medical examiner's office determined in April 2003 that the death was caused by "penetrating sharp force injuries" to the neck. This ruled out the theory that Kent had died of natural causes and was eviscerated by someone hoping to sell the organs.

This horrific crime happened a year and a half ago. The police are still mum on the case. JTR Forums member Dr. Dawn Perlmutter, PhD., one of the world's leading experts on occult ritual crime, was called in to give her observations to the case. To date, she is not at liberty to discuss the case because it is still open.

In addition, this crime has seemingly fallen off the face of the earth, for the most part, in Philadelphia. Daily News writers Jim Nolan and Nicole Weisensee are just about the only interested parties one can approach for updates, and they have none. The police aren't discounting anything, however, as the following incident will attest to.

Immediately after reading this story in the March 1st edition of both Philadelphia papers and after contacting the media by e-mail and phone, I mentioned to one media reporter that it appeared that we may have an occult ritual killing incident here. I also mentioned that author Ivor Edwards had been called in to give advice in the murder of an African boy in London a few years prior. Incredibly, Edwards was contacted by the local Isle Of Wight police, who told him the Philadelphia police department was asking questions about him! As we see, by calling in Dr. Perlmutter and by contacting another criminologist, Edwards, the Philly P.D. is not simply sitting on their hands.

But is the media ? Excluding the few writers who have tackled the case, there has been almost an indecent omission regarding updates to this case, for the public. The similarities between some of the victims attributed to Jack the Ripper and the Badlands' Pete Kent stop where the interest begins. These five women unwillingly were the catalysts to a 116 year investigation that seems inexhaustible, while hardly anyone has heard of Kent.

It's my contention that, had Willie Pete Kent been a suburban white kid seeking to score cocaine in the neighborhood and wound up ripped like Kent did, we would have seen more, a lot more, regarding the case. Had Pete been a public figure, a rabbi, a school teacher, or a member of the mayor's family, the resulting coverage would have been staggering.

There won't be any walks to see where Pete Kent's body was found as there are for Jack the Ripper's victims. The Badlands are still the Badlands, unlike Whitechapel, which has been upgraded. There likewise doesn't seem to be an interest in bringing to light the possible occult nature of this crime, despite having access to one of the world's best authorities on these type of crimes. Is this a case of sweeping the proverbial dirt under the rug ? Only time will tell.

SOURCES:

Begg, Paul, *Jack the Ripper: The Definitive History* 2003

Gibbons Jr., Thomas J., "Occult link investigated in slaying, organ theft" *The Philadelphia Inquirer,* April 5, 2003

Gibbons Jr., "Medical examiner: eviscerated man was murdered" *The Philadelphia Inquirer,* April 10, 2003

Hickey, Brian, "The Remains of the Day" *Philadelphia Weekly,* April 2, 2003

The Whitechapel Letterbox

Dear Dan,

In the latest *RN* [April 2004], Tim [Mosley] writes what appears on the surface to be an objective and unbiased article ["A Ripper Retrospective"] looking at the current breed of Ripper enthusiast, how we view the case as individuals and how we interact with each other. However, Tim ventures more than once into the realm of wild speculation regarding people's primary motives for getting involved, and often uses transparently subjective — even offensive — language to describe certain personalties and what he thinks drives them to contribute their various observations on the subject.

Tim describes Caz, for example, as a 'gadfly', whose only joy in life appears to be 'butting in on private message board exchanges' in an aggressive way, with the aim of making an unpopular nuisance of herself and provoking hostility.

Firstly, it's news to me that any message board exchange appearing in a public forum like the *Casebook* can be considered private. Secondly, why does Tim single me out and accuse me of this strange 'crime', when everyone else is merely joining in a conversation, adding to the discussion in hand, responding to points made by others, offering an opinion of their own, asking a pertinant question, debating along merrily with their fellow posters, or even disagreeing strongly with what someone else has written? And thirdly, what makes Tim think he knows enough about the people he cites to generalise and be so negative about some of them, waxing lyrical as he prejudges my own supposed motivations?

I have thought long and hard about possible explanations for Tim's attitude towards me, none of which would show him in a particularly good light if true. Is it racism? (I'm a Brit.) Is it sexism? (I'm a woman.) Is it elitism? (I'm a nobody and a relative newcomer to the case.) I can't believe any of these prejudices could really be to blame. So is it personal? Has Tim ever felt personally offended by something I have written? Yes, I think he probably has.

Do you remember that I once picked Tim up on the boards about his use of 'literally' in a previous RN article he had written? He wrote something about the victims 'literally' digging their graves with their tongues, and perhaps I should have held mine, but instead I foolishly tried to explain why 'literally' is the total opposite of 'figuratively' or 'metaphorically'. I believe it may have been you who came in after me to support what I wrote. Yet I doubt Tim will ever accuse you of being a gadfly who butts in on private exchanges!

:-)

- Caroline Anne "Caz" Morris

Caz (and readers),

Actually, I think I've been called worse. I'm not going to worry about it, though, since that's in the past.

In fact, I recommend that everyone let go of old conflicts and start fresh. After all, if I had refused to deal with anyone I have ever had a heated argument with in the past, it's safe to say that the vast majority of the contents in this issue wouldn't be here.

I can't speak to the content of previous issues, since I wasn't editor then. Nor is it my place to take sides or make comments without knowing the full situation.

I do, however, promise to try to keep **Ripper Notes** *professional. People can disagree and still remain civil. If I do end up letting something through that any reader objects to, they are free to send a letter and take me to task... but I would hope they would show the same civility and fairness that they expect from me.*

-Dan

'My Funny Litt|e Games'

RELUCTANT HANGMAN   He doesn't want to leave you dangling...

James Berry was called the Reluctant Hangman by some (see book reviews for more on Berry). It's an interesting name, and one that provides a good opportunity for a puzzle based upon the old Hangman game. Here you are out to guess a word or phrase, but instead of making random letter guesses and then drawing in body parts if you are wrong, this hangman gives you clues. The hints give you names of various people, and when you fill in their corresponding aliases or nicknames, the circled line of letters going down spells out the answer.

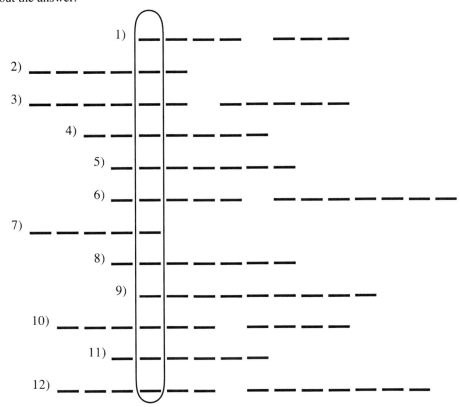

1) Elizabeth Stride   2) Annie Chapman's false last name, based upon occupation of former husband   3) Thomas Bowyer   4) Name Catherine Eddowes gave to police when picked up for being drunk   5) The last name Severin Klosowski took to use as his own from a woman he was involved with   6) Charles Lutwidge Dodgson   7) Ripperologist Adrian Phypers' nickname   8) George Sim's 'nym   9) Edward Stanley, an acquaintance of Annie Chapman, was known as " The _____"   10) Martha Tabram's friend Mary Ann Connelly   11) The last name Catherine Eddowes took temporarily so it would match her common law husband (no, not that one, the other one)   12) PC William Thick's nickname

WALL SCRAWL? Some people see the letters "**FM**" behind Mary Jane Kelly's body in the crime scene photo and use it to support their theories. Well, we're going to use the idea for a puzzle...

```
L  G  K  C  I  R  E
N  L  N  T  H  S  B
I  H  E  C  R  Y  N
M  O  R  E  C  A  O
M  E  L  F  M  C  S
```

This one is kind of like the game Boggle. You try to spell words by going from letter to letter. In this case you can only start with the bold **F** or **M** at the bottom center. Then move either left, right, up, down or diagonal one space, continuing until you finish a word or phrase. You can't use the same letter more than once in the same word or phrase.

For example, to spell the word "meet" you just start at the M, go to the upper left one space, then to the upper left another space and finally to the upper right one space.

But the word "fleece" wouldn't work, because you can't reuse the same E twice in the word and can't skip to another E elsewhere on the board. Once you connect f-l-e-e–c there's no E left to use that's only one space away.

The object here is to find different words or phrases based upon the clues below and following the rules above. When you find one, write them down on the next page. If you come up with other words, you can write them at the bottom. Good luck!

1) What some diary supporters say the FM stands for. 2) What the some conspiracy buffs say the FM stands for. 3) Name of person identified by "the ear and eyes." 4) When Ada Wilson was attacked. 5) Name of a man who wanted money from Mary. 6) Name of man Mary used to date. 7) Name of the person who gave out Lusk's address. 8) Return address of the Lusk letter. 9) Nickname of suspect for Carrie Brown's murder mentioned in Wolf Vanderlinden's article. 10) Name of the doctor on the TV show that had an episode with Jack the Ripper in it mentioned in John Hacker's article. 11) What we wish Mary had gotten from Jack instead of an attack with a knife. 12) What the people who think that the body isn't Mary's say she might have done.

WALL SCRAWL? *Put your answers here:*

1)   2)

3)   4)

5)   6)

7)   8)

9)   10)

11)   12)

Other words found (for fun, they aren't part of the listed answers):

ANSWERS:

Reluctant Hangman

1) Long Liz 2) Siffey, Sievey or Sivvey 3) Indian Harry 4) Nothing 5) Chapman
6) Lewis Carroll 7) Viper 8) Dagonet 9) Pensioner 10) Pearly Poll 11) Conway
12) Johnny Upright   Solution: Leather Apron

Wall Scrawl?

(Abbreviations: R = Right, L = Left, U = Up, D = Down, UR = Up and Right,
UL = Up and Left, DR = Down and Right, DL = Down and Left.)

1) Start at F, move L, UL, R, U, U, DR, D, DR, UR, U, UR, UL, L, L, L
2) Start at F, move UL, U, DR, DR, UR, DR, U, U, UL
3) Start at M, move UR, UL, R
4) Start at M, move UR, UL, L, UR
5) Start at M, move U, DR, U, UL, UL, R, DR (first three moves can also be R, UL, R)
6) Start at F, move L, L, UL, U, U, UR (some people spell the name L, L, L, U, U, U, UR)
7) Start at M, move UR, UL, UR, L
8) Start at F, move UL, L, L, UR, R, UL, UL
9) Start at F, move UL, U, U, DR, UR, DR
10) Start at M, move U, DR, UR, UL
11) Start at M, move UL, UR, D, UR
12) Start at F, move L, UR, UL (that works on its own, but can add L, D, L/DL, DR/E)

Printed in the United States
99135LV00002B/43/A